Maskîkhîwîno

The Medicine Man

Maskikhiwino

The Medicine Man

The Story of a Pioneer Northern Doctor

By

Germain O. Lavoie

Copyright © Germain O. Lavoie

Canadian Cataloguing in Publication Data
    Lavoie, Germain O.

    Maskikhiwino, the Medicine Man
    A story of a pioneer northern doctor raising his family in an   isolated Northern Saskatchewan village from 1934 to 1953.

ISBN 0-9737361
First Nations, Metis, History, Medicine, Biography, Great Depression, early aviation in the north of Canada.

Published and distributed in 2005 by Amyot Lake publishing,
(A division of NSMS.)

Little Amyot Lake
P.O. Box 324 Beauval Saskatchewan S0M 0G0
Phone/Fax 306-288 4661

Printed and bound in Canada by ArtBookbindery.com of Winnipeg, MB

Dedicated to

Joseph Walcer

without whose help this
book would not have been
printed
in this Saskatchewan Centennial
Year.

TABLE OF CONTENTS

Foreword to "Maskkhiwino, the Medicine Man"
By Germain Lavoie

I will not swear to the absolute, 100% historical accuracy of the story that follows. Nostalgia that has been nurtured and ripened for sixty some years may, in the process, compress or expand somewhat, and some details may have been misplaced or mis-recalled. But those aging effects do not substantially put the recollections outside the realm of truth. It is unfortunate that my father, Doctor Philip Ernest Lavoie, did not keep notes on his northern experience. As a consequence I have had to put the story together with information recalled from conversations with my parents and a few written and pictorial sources. As a result, some parts of the text might best be described as "creative non-fiction" and much of the story is mine.

I did depend to some degree on my two older brothers for verification but, to my dismay, they seldom agreed with each other or with me. Inevitably, I chose the version that I found most interesting or readable.

The story is set in the hard years that began during the dirty thirties and ended post WW II. It's a story of a pioneer doctor who went to the still isolated north of Saskatchewan primarily to escape the depression on the dried out prairies but who was to fall in love with a land and a people. That decided him to stay on there rather than to return to the comforts of the south. It is also a story of a boy growing up in a primitive northern village and loving it.

My thanks go out to the many people who encouraged me to get on with the job, especially my wife Jeannie, my daughter Nicole and my son Marton all of whom still are loyal northern residents. I am particularly grateful to Rod MacIntyre, my invaluable mentor, who brought the knowledge of a professional author to my writing. I thank Les MacPherson of the Saskatoon Star Phoenix who, several years ago, saw promise in my writing and in my subject matter and encouraged me to write this story.

2

I owe a debt of gratitude as well to the late Richard
Loeffler of Pahkisimon Nuye-Ah Library System. He gave me
the benefit of his publishing experience by reading and
making suggestions about my earlier chapters, all for the
cost of a lunch. Mr. Greg Rubin at Saskatchewan Health
Resource Centre copied several hundred pages of records
about the Ile a la Crosse hospital from 1934 to 1954 which
proved very helpful.

Lastly I must try to express my heartfelt gratitude to
Doctor Stuart Houston, respected writer, naturalist and
physician who generously proofread my manuscript and gave
it his "Imprimatur". His glowing review appears on the back
cover. For his invaluable service, I say, "Milles mercies,
cher docteur."

Author's note: Naturally as I was still an infant at the beginning of this story I can only tell it through piecing together snippets of information gathered over the years and letting my imagination hold sway. I have tried my best to describe how it came about that my family moved to an isolated northern village in the mid 1930's.I believe it to be close to the way it all began.

CHAPTER 1: - THE DECISION

Doctor Philip Ernest Lavoie sat in the dimly lit passenger car of the train taking him from Prince Albert to Big River Saskatchewan.

The trip from Leader as far as Saskatoon in a friend's automobile had not been very pleasant. His wife Marie-Lourdes had maintained a stony silence the whole voyage, speaking only to three year old Emile and ministering to the baby, Germain, not yet 4 months old, in the rear seat.

The doctor had tried to include her in the conversations he had with his friend John Keelan, the Prelate lawyer, as they drove, but it wasn't difficult for her to feign deafness over the rattle of the beat up Model A Ford.

One topic he had learned to avoid was his intention to go north to Ile a la Crosse Saskatchewan.

Despite her opposition, he had decided to try the government post he had been offered as Medical Superintendent in the small hospital that served a large area of northwestern Saskatchewan. Admittedly he knew very little about what to expect in that region.

He had been told that the whole North was populated by Indian and Métis people with just a sprinkling of white missionaries and Hudson Bay Company employees here and there. From the start, Marie-Lourdes had made her objections to the move very clearly and very loudly between her sobs. Doctor Lavoie didn't want to get her started again in the hearing of his friend. There had been a grudging agreement that she would stay with her sister Gertrude Bourgeois and her husband Albert in Spiritwood until the doctor had, as she put it, regained his senses.

Before his decision to go to that isolated village, the doctor had tried to reason with his wife. She hadn't been swayed even by the fact that it was her distant cousin, Roman Catholic Bishop Martin Lajeunesse, who had written to suggest the possibility of the job. To her, leaving their newest home in Leader and going to such a desolate place so far away, a place probably still populated by wild savages, was incomprehensible.

How could he even consider it, her with a new baby and little Emile to look after? And what would happen to the other two children? Cecile, the oldest at the age of 16, was in her last year at the convent in Ponteix. The second child, seven year old René had just been re-enrolled in the boarding school in Gravelbourg. If she were to go to this far off place would she ever see them again?

The Lavoie family had been met at the Saskatoon train station by Gertrude and her talkative husband, Albert Bourgeois. As pre-arranged the Bourgeois were to take Marie-Lourdes and the two infants on to Spiritwood where Albert was the principal of the small school. The farewell between the doctor and his red-eyed spouse had been strained as he boarded the train to Prince Albert where he would connect with the train to Big River.

Doctor Lavoie had been forced to face some harsh realities. The harshest was that there seemed to be no end to the soul wrenching depression on the prairies. 1934 in Leader had been no better than either Laflêche or Montmartre had been in the four previous years of prairie drought. The dry winds relentlessly lifted the prairie dirt so high that it often darkened the southern

Saskatchewan skies, blotting out much of the sun's light but none of its heat.

The poverty stricken farmers and their families who were trapped inexorably beneath that dust cloud still got sick and continued to need a doctor's help. The fact that they could pay neither for his services nor for the medicines that he had to provide from his private dispensary had brought him to the brink of bankruptcy. How was he to pay the tuition costs of his two older children's boarding schools? Why couldn't Marie-Lourdes understand the desperate financial straits that they were in and recognize what a Godsend an assured monthly income in a government position would be?

He shook his head at the irony of the early September snowflakes streaming by the train window to form small snowdrifts between the banks of dust that shadowed each telegraph post. Was Mother Nature playing a last mean joke on him as he tried to escape her bony clutch?

He awoke with a start as the conductor shook his shoulder to announce the Big River Station.

Clutching his medical bag in one hand and his tattered valise in the other, he made his way in the darkness to the small clap-board hotel across from the station. He paid the dollar room charge in the full knowledge that he was being gouged. He only asked to be awakened before seven the next morning when arrangements had been made for the Saskatchewan Air Patrol pilot to pick him up.

In the September dawn he barely had time for a quick gulp of weak coffee and a bite of dry unbuttered toast when a man in an aviator's helmet and goggles yelled at him from the café door.

"You Doc Leviole?"

"Yes I am Doctor Lavoie. Are you the one who will take me to Ile a la Crosse?"

"Yeah. But we'd better get a wiggle on because it looks like maybe more snow coming."

So saying he led the way to the battered truck into which he carelessly threw the doctor's bag and grip.

"It is far to the airstrip?" The doctor wanted to know.

"Ain't no airstrips in the North, Doc", the pilot answered.

"We'll be taking off from the Ladder Lake Float Base and, hopefully, we'll land on Ile-a-la-Crosse Lake before it freezes over".

The road to Ladder Lake was nothing more than two rough ruts through the bush. The Doctor's first sight of the flimsy looking aircraft tied up to the floats made his gorge rise. They looked like small boats that awkwardly supported two wings and a rearward facing engine.

He was to feel even less at ease as the pilot strapped a parachute onto his back and explained,

"These Vickers Vedettes are pretty dependable machines but if something happens and we have to jump, count to three after you jump and pull on this handle to open the chute."

"But what if we are over a lake?" the doctor objected. "I can't swim."

"That'll be your funeral, not mine Doc. She's all gassed up and ready to go so climb into the front cockpit and we'll take off." The pilot seemed totally unconcerned about his passenger's obvious nervousness.

As they gathered take off speed on the water, Doctor Lavoie gripped the edge of the cock-pit so hard that his bloodless fingers felt frozen in place.

And finally, as he felt his stomach drop, he sensed that the machine was rising but realized that his eyes were tightly closed.

Cautiously,   he opened them but it took him some time before he was brave enough to look around and down.

What he saw astonished him. There seemed to be almost as much water as there was land. Jump? Oh no!

He would stay in his mechanical hole no matter what might happen.

A *VICKERS VEDETTE IN FLIGHT OVER THE NORTH*

Gradually, he relaxed a bit and was able to free his hands. How slowly the terrain seemed to move below them. Only later, when he caught a glimpse of the plane's shadow racing across the muskegs and tree tops, did he become aware of their speed.

What a beautiful vista was revealed as the fall mist melted before the rising sun. And so much water! He had not seen such expanses since he had left his boyhood home near the Gulf of Saint Laurence. The further they flew, the bigger the lakes and rivers seemed to become.

After what seemed like an eternity, the pilot banked his aircraft so steeply over yet another big lake that the doctor once more grabbed the cockpit edge in fright as the world tilted crazily beneath him. But he kept his eyes open and caught a brief glimpse of a tiny church surrounded by a scattering of tiny houses all seemingly surrounded by water. Was this Lilliputian place to be his new home?

Ile a la Crosse from the air. The wing struts resemble those of a Vedette.

The world regained its balance as the lake's surface rushed up to meet them. The floatplane skimmed then settled onto the semi-solid comfort of water. The doctor had survived his first flight.

The pilot cut his engine and coasted in to the wooden dock near the church. He held the wing struts as Doctor Lavoie cautiously made his way up to the dock on cramped legs.

"S'pose you'll be wantin' to go to the hospital first," the pilot said as he retrieved his passenger's bags. "It's that low building behind the church."

"Thank you very much for our safe arrival," the doctor ventured. "Now about your charges."

"All taken care of by the government Forestry Service. Good luck Doc. Don't lose your scalp, ha ha."

With that the pilot pushed out into the lake. As the doctor walked towards his new life he heard the engine roar and turned to watch as the craft skimmed the water for a long distance before gradually lifting up into the heavens.

As he drew near the little hospital, he noted it needed painting but the grounds were neat and the wooden steps leading up to the entrance were worn but sturdy.

As soon as he stepped through the doorway he recognized the unmistakable habit of a Grey Nun who was talking to a woman with a kerchief over her hair.

"Bonjour ma Soeur. Je suis le nouveau docteur."

At this greeting little Sister Gaudette turned and throwing her arms up exclaimed, "Mon Doux Seigneur! Il parle français!" (My sweet Lord. He speaks French.)

Her obvious delight at his arrival immediately set the doctor at ease.

"Soeur Supérieure! Venez voir.", she called to another nun all dressed in nursing white. C'est le nouveau docteur et il parle français."

It was evident from this stress on the doctor's linguistic ability that the previous MD had not been able to speak French.

Sister Boisvert, the superior, took over the welcoming ceremonies, showing the new arrival first to his office where he left his coat, cap and bags.

As they walked the hallways with the two nuns firing questions and information at him, the doctor saw a number of patients timidly peeking out of their hospital rooms.

"Awina ana?' they asked one another in loud whispers who this gentleman was.

"Maskihkiwino itikwe" a medicine man maybe, one of them guessed.

"Aha, ahpo itikwe" Yes, that's possible others agreed.

"Peyakwan maskihkiwiyinew ispahkosiw" a woman patient verified the identification noting that, indeed, he smelled like a medicine man.

Finally the new arrival was ushered into the adjoining convent refectory where he was offered a meal of reheated stew in which the potatoes and turnips were still cold in the centre. But as his single bite of dry toast of the early morning had done nothing to satisfy his hunger, he relished every morsel, wiping his plate clean with the delicious home made bread that had been provided.

As he ate, there was a constant stream of other nuns coming in to see this welcome stranger for themselves. Little Sister Gaudette played the part of mistress of ceremonies, having been the first to meet him, giving one and all the story of her astonishing discovery that "le Docteur Lavoie parle français."

This excited hubbub was interrupted by the arrival of Père Rossignol, the head priest of the Mission Saint Jean Baptiste. After welcoming the doctor the Father offered to show him through the smallish cottage near the side entrance of the hospital, the residence reserved for the Medical Superintendent.

Rather grandly, the good father snapped on the light explaining that the house was connected to the hospital electrical and running water systems noting that not even the rectory enjoyed these luxuries.

The doctor noted the huge fireplace of fieldstones in the parlor but was immediately assured that there was a wood furnace in the cellar and the kitchen wood-stove was plumbed to a hot water tank.

The "piece de resistance" was evidently the three piece bathroom in which the missionary seemed to want to linger for quite some time.

CHAPTER 2:- THE PICTURE

Marie-Lourdes Lavoie was restless. She kept putting down her embroidery to stare out of the window at the wintry scene of early January 1935. Even though it was only four o'clock, it was already quite dark and she knew that soon little Emile would be coming home from the Spiritwood kindergarten holding her niece's hand. This niece, her namesake Marie-Lourdes, had taken a liking to the four year old and the feeling was mutual. She always accompanied the little boy to and from school and seemed to delight in showing his latest crayon drawings to the rest of the Bourgeois children and to "tante Gertrude'.

Just then, as if on signal, the elder Marie-Lourdes heard the baby stir in his borrowed crib where she had put him down for his afternoon nap. It was uncanny how an eight month old infant seemed to sense that his cousin "Mou-Lou" would soon be there to play with him and his brother, "Mil". He would get so excited that it was difficult for his mother to change his diaper. He kept repeating "Mou-Lou, Mou-Lou, Mou-lou" until the girl would open the bedroom door and take him out of his little bed.

Then it was time for all the children to

play a game of chase on all fours in the
parloir while waiting for supper to be
served.Baby Germain would scream in delight
when one of his cousins caught him and
tickled his tummy.

In the peace and quiet of her room,
Marie-Lourdes Lavoie reread several of her
husband's letters. In spite of the irregular
mail service to and from the North, quite a
bit of correspondence had been exchanged
between the two.

From his letters to her, it was obvious
that the doctor had become enchanted by this
new and lush environment. All that water!
And there was fresh fish and game on the
table to go with the vegetables and canned
berries supplied by the Catholic Mission
which operated the Saint Joseph Hospital.

He wrote of the friendliness of the
missionary priests, brothers and sisters and
of the quiet dignity and good manners of the
Métis residents of the hamlet, many of whom
spoke passable French.

He described his work which had required
him to visit several outposts by motorized
canoe. Then when the lakes and rivers were
frozen in November, he had even experienced
riding behind a dog team with a native
driver. And he had overcome his fear of
flying, particularly when the aircraft's
floats had given way to skis. Evidently,
wearing a parachute while flying over solid

ice had at least relieved his mind about the possibility of drowning.

Madame Lavoie's replies, full of recriminations at first, gradually mollified in tone. Welcome as she had been made to feel by her sister Gertrude's family, she couldn't help reminiscing about how pleasant her life had been when she had been mistress of her own house, in keeping with her station as a doctor's wife.

She wrote about brother-in-law Albert's incessant jokes, many at her expense, and she worried that the baby Germain's fussing might be annoying the Bourgeois children.

The loneliness of that 1934 Christmas away from her husband had caused her to soften somewhat her adamant stand against going to Ile a la Crosse to join "le docteur" as she always called him. But perhaps there was more to her change of heart than pure loneliness.

The doctor had always considered himself a bit of a photographer. Proud owner of a big box camera, he often sent films to Spiritwood to be developed, which Albert Bourgeois was happy to get done, curious as he himself was about all things northern. One particular photograph had caught everyone's attention. It showed the doctor with three other people standing in front of an aeroplane on skis. One man with a full beard and wearing his black cassock beneath his winter jacket was obviously a missionary priest. The man in the aviator's cap would be the pilot. It was seeing the woman standing beside the doctor that intrigued and delighted Albert. This lady's fancy footwear and stylish hat and coat clearly indicated that she was not a nun.

Pictured L-R, Rev. Father Moreaud, Dr. Lavoie, Nurse Jeanne Pogu and pilot "Dutch" Holland. Aircraft: A Fairchild?

Nurse Pogu was, in fact, one of only two non-religious nurses at Saint Joseph Hospital and it became evident from the doctor's letters that she sometimes accompanied him on his flights to treat or to evacuate distant patients.

She was quite attractive and as a result became the centre of Albert's teasing of his sister-in-law, Marie-Lourdes.

With a straight face, he would insinuate how lucky she was that her husband was a good Catholic, not at all given to sinful thoughts of infidelity. But then, in that lonely and cold place, it would take the strength of a saint to resist the temptations of the flesh, Albert opined. The butt of his teasing laughed it off, but there was no denying the uneasy feelings that the photo had awakened in her.

Whatever the reason for her capitulation, Marie-Lourdes Lavoie sat down on that January evening and wrote to the doctor asking him to arrange her travel to Ile a la Crosse.

CHAPTER 3: - A FAMILY REUNITED

AUTHOR'S NOTE: So this is the point when I can take over telling the story because from now on I am in the middle of it. I am also identified as the maskikhiwino okossissa, the medicine man's son, from the moment of my arrival in Ile a la Crosse.

It was in mid-February of 1935 when I was nine months old that my mother and I arrived. Naturally I can't pretend that I was yet aware of everything that was going on at that early age, but my history and our history as a northern family begins then, and telling that story is the purpose of this book.

From the moment I could talk and walk, I was full of questions and curiosity. Thus I was to record my mother's description of our journey to the north as she explained it to Nurse Evangeline Russell in our kitchen one day. It was common knowledge that my mother and Nurse Pogu had not hit it off too well and that lady resigned soon after mother and I arrived.

Her eventual replacement, Nurse Russel, or Evange as she was known for short, got into the habit of visiting Madame Lavoie twice a day so she could sneak a cigarette out of sight of the nuns. As Evange's French was worse than my mother's English, my mother, hereinafter called Maman, was forced to trot out her broken English to carry on a conversation with her friend.

It was during one of these smoke breaks that the story of our mid-winter journey north was told. I will try to render her description of our first flight just as she told it in her own words.

"My sister her 'usband say 'e's know a man in Shellbrooke who 'ave a aeroplan from de war an' maybe 'e could take me an de bébé for not ver' much monies. Petit Emile could stay with Gertrude's family to finish school in Spiritwood. So I'm say it is good. It was winter tam, febvrier, but we went to Shellbrooke an' dat man say 'e will take me. So nex' day we go to dat place where de aeroplan was. De machine 'ave skis for de snow an two, how you say "ailes", yes, wings, and two 'oles wit'out couvertures."

"Mon Dieux, I was scare'. But de pilote is say get in de 'ole in front under de wing and hold de bébé on my knees. So I did dat. Den de pilote is go in front and turn de propelleur until de hingine is start, den he go in de hole in de back an' pretty soon we go fas' and jomp in de sky. It make so much de noise I cannot 'ear de bébé if he is cry. An' I was so cole an' so scare' an' de bébé is peepee an' me too I peepee my pants. So I say my rosairie all de way to Ile a la Crosse where we lan' on de ice in front of de church".

Above is a picture of a rebuilt Pheasant F10 which may be the type of aircraft we flew Feb. 1935.

I believe that may have been the only time in her nearly 20 years of living there that Maman felt anything akin to happiness to be in Ile a la-Crosse. From the moment her heart had stopped its fright induced racing and she had warmed herself somewhat at the wood stove in the small kitchen of the doctor's house, she longed to return to civilisation, preferably to L'Annonciation Quebec, her childhood home.

Her husband didn't notice her disappointment right away so taken up was he with hugging his youngest child, me. But it didn't take Maman long to point out the failings of the doctor's residence.

The list was extensive. Not only was the kitchen small but it had very little in the way of cupboard and counter space. The table was over a trapdoor leading to the cellar and had to be moved out of the way every time the doctor needed to descend the steps to feed the wood furnace.

The room next to the kitchen, purportedly meant to be the dining room, also was so tiny that she doubted that her 8 piece dining set, including the glass front china cabinet, would fit in there. That set, a wedding gift from her father and mother, she had absolutely refused to sell through all their moves. It was then stored in a barn owned by her sister Marie-Anne's husband, Elzear Viens.

The fairly large living room with its big stone fire-place generated no comment. Not so the only bedroom with adjoining bathroom. Where were the children to sleep when they came home from boarding school? In fact where was the baby to sleep? On the sofa in the living room? There was hardly enough space for a crib in the one bedroom.

In this view of the Roman Catholic Mission, the Doctor's one bedroom house and St. Joseph's Hospital are in the foreground.

It was obvious that the residence had not been built with a family in mind. In fact, the previous medical doctor had opted to stay in a room in the hospital where he resided only part time, regularly going south to continue private practice and to be with his family.

The doctor assured his wife that he would talk to Father Rossignol, the mission superior, about necessary housing improvements immediately to allay her worries. Meanwhile, he led Maman to the hospital to introduce her to the Grey Nuns.

As he expected, these good ladies were effusive in their welcome and each had to have her turn of holding the baby. They insisted that Madame Lavoie join them in the refectory for tea while the doctor went to talk to Père Rossignol.

Soon he and Frère Landry, the mission carpenter, were looking at the house to see what might be done to accommodate the doctor's family. They agreed that a two bedroom wing could be added and, at the doctor's insistence, a pantry cum utility room extension would increase the kitchen's meagre storage capacity.

Perhaps the mission superior might have been positively influenced by the discovery that Madame Lavoie was somehow related to his boss, the bishop. But frankly, he was so happy to have a Catholic doctor again at the mission that he sensed that if the housing improvements encouraged the doctor to stay on, it would be worth the expenditure.

Our house near the hospital complete with two additions separated by the two chimneys.

And so when the frost had left the ground in mid-May, the building modifications were begun and the project was completed by the end of June 1935.

That's when the doctor flew to Prince Albert and set about gathering the rest of his family. Borrowing Albert Bourgeois old "Whippet" automobile, he picked up René in Gravelbourg, Cecile in Ponteix where they were joined by Gabrielle Senechal, Marie-Lourde's widowed younger sister. They avoided Regina where it was rumoured there was a lot of tension because of the"On to

Ottawa" gang of unemployed trekkers who were stalled there by federal government action.

They returned to Leader Saskatchewan where Doc sold whatever belongings he had left there the previous year in the care of his friend. In no position to haggle he accepted whatever he was offered. This included our house which also had contained his medical office and dispensary.

This done, the doctor loaded all our furniture and clothing on the train to Big River which he boarded along with my seventeen year old sister, Cécile, and my two older brothers, René and Emile, aged eight and five respectively. "Tante Gabi", as aunt Gabrielle was familiarly known, had agreed to go along to look after the kids.

Pictured above are two contrasting forms of northern freight carriers; a wooden scow tied to the same wharf as a "JUNKERS BOXCAR" aeroplane that was used very rarely because of the cost.

From Big River, Doctor Lavoie, by now an experienced air traveller, flew back to

Ile-a-la-Crosse with five year old Emile on his lap. The rest of the party caught the early summer freight barges that floated down the Cowan River, into the Beaver River and unloaded supplies at various Churchill River system communities, including the recognized capital of the Northwest, Ile a la Crosse.

How I wish I had been old enough to have shared in that floating adventure but my father had left me with my mother in Ile a la Crosse. Lucky René had the time of his life on the scow while Cecile and "Tante" Gabi, expecting to be attacked or drowned at any minute, cowered on the load. The eventual reunion of all the family on the shore of Lac Ile-a-la-Crosse was, I imagine, a very noisy affair with everybody talking and crying at once, as French-Canadians tend to do.

Tante Gabi and Cécile helped Maman set up her expanded house that summer of '35, never quite overcoming the fear for their lives as instilled by Marie-Lourde's repeated warnings. By contrast, René and Emile spent an idyllic summer playing with their new Métis and Indian friends, and learning their first delicious Cree swear words.

But come September, Tante Gabi took Cécile to Regina where she had been accepted for Medical Lab Technician training. Eight year old René and Emile, still just five, were enrolled in Jardin de l'Enfance, the

boarding school in Gravelbourg. Emile
can't recall how they got there, but I'm
certain that René told me later that they
had gone by canoe to Beauval and went to
Meadow Lake from there by horse and wagon
along the rough wagon trail that followed
the Beaver River south. From Meadow Lake,
they had boarded the North Battleford bus
south with connections there to Regina for
Cecile and to Gravelbourg for the boys.

CHAPTER 4:- DOC ADAPTS TO NORTHERN REALITY

Now that he had his family comfortably settled, Doctor Lavoie felt free to throw himself zealously into his work, travelling to all parts of his vast district.

For he was not limited to the hospital but was responsible for the health of native people from as far south as Green Lake to as far north as Camsell Portage, Goldfields and Fond du Lac on Athabasca Lake.

He travelled to places like Patuanak, Canoe Lake, Buffalo Narrows and Beauval by freighter canoe with a native guide until freeze-up. In winter he often sat in a toboggan behind a team of half wild dogs. His minuscule budget did allow him to charter aircraft to his more distant villages such as La Loche, Dipper, Snake Lake (now Pinehouse), and the Athabasca Basin. He did everything that his medical skill and isolation dictated, from removing appendices to pulling decayed teeth.

NOTE: This is the only picture we could find of Doc in his toboggan. Rene recognized Montagnais' dogs and Doc's favorite cap.

He was soon to show his ability to overcome medical challenges peculiar to the northern context. In fact, about two months after Maman and I arrived, Doctor Lavoie and the hospital staff saved the life of one Joseph Eugene Burnouf, a French expatriate who had brought his near genius building skills to primitive Saskatchewan at the turn of the century. The event is best described by the doctor himself in an article he wrote hoping the southern press might print it. Here it is as taken verbatim from his carbon copy.

First Major Surgical Operation North of Latitude 55*

On Easter Monday the 22nd of April (1935) the hospital of Ile a la Crosse was the theatre for the first major surgical operation ever done in that far isolated part of the Province. J.E.Burnouf well known and esteemed trader of Beauval and Ile a la Crosse was operated upon in emergency for a strangulated hernia. It was, at this time of breakup, impossible to take him out either by airplane or other means of travel, to a better equipped surgical centre. So the local staff of the hospital rolled up their sleeves and got busy. The important question of sterilization attracted first attention. The hospital is equipped with sterilizers, but no steam; the boiler of the heating plant being out of commission since 1930. However the difficulty was eliminated. A small Auto-Clave was used. Slow it is true but it served the purpose. That emergency case happened during the night. So another difficulty presented itself. There was no adequate light, the electric light plant being also out of commission.

Howevei a couple of gasoline lamps were secured from the Settlement. Finally everything was ready at midnight. Sister Gaudet took charge of the Anaesthesia, and Nurse Rapita assisted Dr. P.E. Lavoie, the present medical superintendent. The operation was successful although quite complicated on account of adhesions caused by a duration of twelve years and the wear of a truss. However with a limited equipment and personnel, everything went well; the patient rallied splendidly, and today, the eighth day after the operation, he is considered well out of danger. A remarkable fact is that in spite of all the difficulties encountered in the preparation of the operation, the patient was operated upon eight hours only after the strangulation. This early intervention beyond a doubt saved Burnouf's life.

The hospital of Ile a la Crosse was erected in 1927 by the Department of Indian Affairs Ottawa, and is supported jointly by the same department and the Department of Public Health of the Province of Saskatchewan.

The hospital and Settlement lie 55'25, Lat. North, and 107'50 Long. West,; or to use the language of the prairies,Township 74, Range 13, west of the third meridian. This hospital of 25 beds is doing a lot of good for hundreds of miles around, and is well appreciated by the population who is(sic) denied the benefits of Civilisation.

The staff consists of Dr, P.E. Lavoie, Medical Superintendent, Rev. Sister Gaudet, Head Nurse, Sister Lavoie, Dietition, Nurse Miss Ann Rapitta, and Mrs Senechale. (END)

The item was indeed picked up by southern and even some eastern newspapers, considerably edited such that it lost some of its northern flavour but it won the acclaim of the medical fraternity. A much abridged version of the event appeared in THE CANADIAN DOCTOR magazine of October 1935.

The doctor was to learn that illnesses which were not considered particularly serious in the South might be a death knell to northern aboriginals who lacked the anti-bodies that people of European stock had developed over the centuries.

For example, in 1937, an outbreak of German measles carried away a quarter of the youngsters who became infected. Even a number of adult native people who became infected died. The hospital was so full of the sick that some had to be made to lie on pallets in the hallways. The nursing staff had to be supplemented by the few white ladies in the hamlet as they would be immune. Doc had to content himself for some two weeks with occasional cat-naps on the examination table in his office.

In no time the epidemic spread to Beauval and Snake Lake. The doctor had to order the closing of the residential schools in his area and to advise parents who came to get their children to camp out with them rather than risk spreading the infection to other villages. Parents were advised to control the high fevers that were common to the illness with regular doses of aspirin and bathing with cold wet cloths.

There were so many deaths that the missionaries had to resort to multiple funerals while the religious brothers had to work full time constructing caskets.

Register of Deaths, Saint Mary Magdalene Church, Beauval Sask

Number of deaths recorded for the period of February 1st to March 31st, 1937 as a result of an epidemic of measles.

Total number of deaths all ages= 67
Of which 49 were children under 14 years of age.

Note that Beauval's population at that time is estimated as less than 200 people including children in the residential school.

Register of Deaths, Saint Jean Baptiste Church, Ile a la Crosse Sask. est. population in 1937, 400.

Number of deaths recorded in the same period as a result of the measles epidemic

Total number of deaths all ages=95
Of which number 63 were children under 14 years of age.

When the epidemic was finally over, parents who had lost children adopted the children of parents who had died. Such are the survival instincts of northern natives.

Doc had to struggle for some time with sub-standard hospital facilities but gradually things improved. In an issue of <u>The Island Breezes,</u> a little news magazine published monthly by the Ile a la Crosse school, he wrote;

I recall also the ruined condition of the Hospital {when I arrived}, property of the Government at the time, absolutely abandoned by neglect to its natural death. Seeing the dilapidated lighting plant, the burst heating system and sewers, one could not but admire

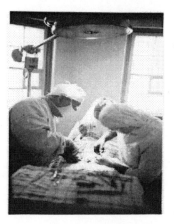

the courage and tenacity of the Missionaries and the Grey Nuns to keep open an institution which was an absolute necessity in a country having then no outlet to an hospital center. The Roman Catholic Bishop of these northern missions took it to himself to make it survive.

Dr. Lavoie, Nursing Sister Boisvert and Nurse Evangeline Russel in the "new" surgery, 1942.

I relive also the amount of patience and coaxing we had to use to break the apathy and antipathy of the Indians. To combat their fear of the hospital, which they considered like a jail, to demonstrate to them the amount of good we could do to them, it took years, lots of patience and lots of kindness.

We   finally   succeeded and in 1940, right in the middle of the war, a three story fire-proof extention had to be erected at the cost of $50,000. It was furnished with heating and lighting plants, laundering facilities, modern Xray, surgical equipment, etc. In fact {now} St. Joseph's has the equipment of a city hospital.(Island Breezes Vol XIV, May 1953)

CHAPTER 5-THE MEDICINE MAN'S SON FITS IN

Emile, Bebe and Maman with the Saint
Jean Baptiste Church in the background.

As for me, like it was for my dad, the
North was a place of wonder and delight.
From the moment I was allowed outside, I was
given free run of the mission. As I learned
to talk, I mixed French and Cree with
abandon and everywhere I went with my curly

blond hair, I was pampered as the "P'ti Mestigosiew", the little Frenchman, by the native ladies. I learned to relish caribou stew, boiled whitefish and, my favourite treat, dried moose meat. Maman, when she saw me coming home avidly chewing on the latter, was convinced it was a chunk of offal I had picked up off the ground and she would snatch it away. I soon learned to finish my dried meat treat before going home.

So it is that I grew up among the natives of the North and came to regard this part of Saskatchewan as my home.

It was a great life and I loved every minute of it. I recall the excitement when the winter supply teams from down south followed the chain of frozen rivers and lakes that led into the primitive North. They delivered the things the bush could not provide; flour, sugar, salt, tea, bacon and even canned fruit. Peaches in the tin seemed so much tastier than home canned blueberries and raspberries by that time of year.

The horse train also carried parcels ordered from the Eatons or the Simpsons catalogues, hopefully arriving just in time for Christmas. It depended on whether we had had a "good early freeze" without too much snow so the ice was thick enough to permit some twenty teams and bob-sleds to travel together in single file from Big River on winter trails without breaking through the ice, which sometimes happened. At the first sight of the sleigh train, all the bigger boys and girls in the village would rush out onto the frozen lake to meet the horses. Then they would either climb on some of the loads for a ride in, or "bumper shine" behind the sleigh runners.

I also have dim memories of my father holding me on a fence post by our yard gate as hundreds of woodland caribou crossed the isthmus of Ile-a-la-Crosse, sometimes even between our house and the hospital. My brother René, when he came home from boarding school for the Christmas holidays, convinced me that these were "Père Noel's"(i.e. Santa Claus's) reindeer that had run away so that he wouldn't be able to deliver toys that year.

But Santa always seemed to make it even if the horse train failed to arrive in time. Aircraft came more and more into regular use in the north delivering mail and, great heavens, booze! "Doc", as my father became more familiarly known by his northern friends, learned that when Cece McNeil or Ernie Buffa wagged their wings over the hospital as they came in for a landing on the lake, there was a special parcel of "medicinal spirits" on board for him. Ah, how my Maman would fret.

CHAPTER 6: - THE BLACKROBES VERSUS SATAN.

No one would ever accuse Doc of being overly religious, but he kept the basic tenets of the Catholic faith without going overboard.

Maman, on the other hand, had to restrain herself from genuflecting whenever she met a priest or a nun on the road. On the odd occasion when one or more religious actually dropped in to our home for a visit, she would go into such a paroxysm of delighted servitude that King George VI would not have created a greater to-do. Out would come the dainty china cups and matching saucers and those special English biscuits that we boys knew meant a real scolding if we so much as opened the tin's lid just for a look. Finally, when the visitors were permitted to refuse yet another cup of tea and prepared to leave, they were fairly swamped with gratitude and curtsies.

Doc's attitude to things or persons reverential was far more measured. He watched his language a bit more carefully and kept to safe topics of conversation such as the weather, the potato crop or the quality and quantity of the winter's wood supply.

But under stress, Doc was not ashamed to call upon the powers of heaven for help, sometimes   with bellowing insistence.

He probably shocked the nursing sisters in the operating room by the force of his "orisons" many times. His favourite saints were Joseph, after whom the hospital was named, and Luke, the patron saint of physicians.

"Maudi-t-affaire Saint Joseph," he might say, "veux-tu bien venir m'aider avec ceci?" (Darn it all St. Joseph, will you come here and help me with this?) Poor little Sister Boisvert, the surgery nurse, wasn't used to having the saints addressed in such a familiar fashion, but she marvelled at how often the "prayer" would help with the surgical procedure.

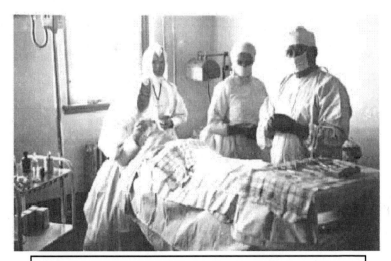

Doc and three Nurses operating in the surgical room.

As for me, from my earliest memory, I was aware that Satan was out to get me if he could. And if I didn't watch myself, the earth might yawn open beneath me to drop me into his fiery domain forever. But if I obeyed Maman, said my prayers and went to church regularly, the strange men who wore black dresses, like women did, would keep the old horned demon at bay.

So, rain or shine, ninety above or forty below, on Sunday, we got dressed up and went to church. Some of the experience was appealing. The priest who said Mass wore a white dress instead of the drab black, and he wore some shiny colourful kind of apron thing over the whole works. Strange to say, most of the time he spoke in some sort of magical language that I guessed only God could understand.

Maman seemed to know a few words that she read out of a little book she always took to church along with her rosary beads.

Mamam's Missal in French and Latin

Saint Jean Baptiste Church in the 30's. The poplar trees in front were about the only trees left on the Ile a la Crosse isthmus at the time.

The part I liked best was the singing. I spent most of my time looking backwards and upwards to where the singers were on a big shelf that had been built at the back of the church, just for them I thought. I was particularly drawn into the contest between "Pé'Père", (my grandfather who had been driven by the depression to join us in Ile a la Crosse), and a Métis called Montagnais (Leon Gardiner) to see who could sing the loudest. When the two of them really got going, the nuns and native women in the choir could hardly be heard. Most of the time I thought Pé'Père had won, but I might have been a bit biased. For some reason, Maman kept turning my head to face the front during these singing matches, which spoiled the fun somewhat.

As for the rest of the service, I found it quite boring, particularly when the white robed priest faced the people and spoke to them for a long, long time, not in the magic language but first in French and then in Cree. It was hard not to fidget at that time. It must have been tough for two other little boys who always sat right behind us because they too kept being shushed by their mothers just as Maman did me. I came to think that these two were called Ponota and Cowiya. It was only after I had mastered Cree that I recognised the words to mean, "be quiet" and "don't do that". In turn, they probably thought my real name might be "soit tranquille" or "fait pas ça".

As little kids of either sex, we always had to sit in the left hand benches with the women while all the men and older boys sat on the right side of the church. The women's side was usually quite packed tight whereas there always seemed to be lots of room on the men's side. That was where Doc sat with René and Emile if they were home from boarding school. Doc often joked that the priests ensured that no "hanky-panky" went on during the service through this separation of the sexes. Only at their wedding ceremony were a man and woman allowed to sit within touching distance of each other, and that was only because they were right in front where the celebrant could keep his eye on the two of them.

Furthermore, all the native women wore heavy black shawls over their heads throughout the service. This garment was worn in such a way as to hide the identity of the wearer from every direction except directly from the front. This was probably meant as a further precaution against any prurient looks from the men's side.

Maman, however, flouted this dress code with impunity and wore all manner of goofy concoctions on her head, much to my embarrassment. I suppose she got away with it because no one was drawn into sinful thoughts by the view of her practically naked head.

Finally all the adults and older kids were allowed to go up to the fence that divided them from God's front yard and after kneeling down in a long row along this fence, each received a little white biscuit. I wasn't allowed to go and get one and I always assumed that was because I had done something to make God, or maybe the priest, angry with me.

Three Lavoie Boys dressed for Church.

Still, I welcomed this procession to the fence because I knew that the service would soon be over and we could all go home to get out of our uncomfortable church clothes and have the customary crêpe brunch. These pancakes were laced with real maple syrup sent to us poor, deprived people by

relatives in Quebec. Personally,   I
preferred the thick corn syrup that the
native women poured on their fried bannock
concoctions   called   "les   beignes".
Occasionally, we had birch tree syrup made
by the missionary brothers who tapped the
trees every spring on L'Ile aux Bouleaux
(Birch Island). The latter seemed a bit
bitter to me and lacked the sweetness level
I preferred. But any gift from the Mission
was treated like a treasure by Maman who
usually reserved the gift syrup for special
guests like Judge Lucier whenever he free-
loaded bed and breakfast from us during his
court tours. I noted that His Honour used
the birch syrup very sparingly despite his
effusive expressions of delight.

But I digress from the battle between
Satan and the men in black robes.

On one particular sunny summer morning,
Maman fussed with my pre-church preparations
even more than usual. Even Doc put on his
best three piece suit and fedora hat. As for
Maman, what a chapeau! Was she trying to
attract bumblebees with all those pretend
flowers?

Finally, we started walking towards the
church and I noted right away that there was
something special in the air. There were
flags and pendants every where. Perhaps that
explained why Maman had denuded her flower

garden of all her prized gladiolas and mums the day before. Were we going to have a big birthday party for someone?

When we got to the front doors of the church, people were all milling around excitedly but nobody was going inside. And some of the men had their shotguns and rifles with them. Was it to be a war instead of a party? Maybe that bad man, Hitler himself, was on the way. But why put up decorations for him? I stood in total confusion as Ponota and Cowiya ran around playing tag. I wasn't allowed to join the game, however, as Maman kept tight hold of my hand.

At last, we heard an aeroplane fly over and bank for a landing near Big Island. Was it a bomber? From its loud roar it sounded very much like a warplane might sound. I feared the worst as the men began loading their guns and rifles. I expected Maman would drag me away into the safety of the church and I would miss all the fighting. But she didn't. In fact, rather than look scared, she appeared joyous.

Finally, we could hear the plane as it approached the mission wharf. When the engine stopped, the men cocked their weapons and made ready to repel whatever enemy was at hand.

But instead, they pointed their guns skyward and started shooting haphazardly through the poplar branches of the only grove of trees left alive on the isthmus, right in front of the church.

The noise was deafening and because Maman still held one hand, I could only cover one ear and I began to cry in fear.

Noting my tears, Doc picked me up and tried to calm me. "Mais qu'est-ce qu'ils veulent tuer la haut?" I asked him, convinced the men must be trying to kill something dangerous up there that might attack us.

Doc merely laughed at my questions and assured me, "C'est seulement un 'feu-de-joix' pour Monseigneur, he said. "N'a pas peur mon p'ti gars." (It is just a fusillade of joy for his Lordship. Don't be afraid my little one.)

As Doc didn't seem afraid, I heeded his suggestion to calm my terror. A "fire of joy" for someone called Monseigneur? Who was that who could deserve such a loud reception? Finally, I saw a stranger in a  black robe making his way through the crowd. He looked different from the other blackrobes though. He wore a purple sash around his waist and a matching beanie on his head and a whole row of purple buttons down the front of his dress.

Bishop lajeunesse having his ring kissed by some children.

And as this grand personage approached the church, people kept kneeling down in front of him and actually seemed to be kissing his hand.

Finally there he was in front of us.

"Bonjour Docteur. Et cousine Marie-Lourdes. Tu vas biens?" he greeted my parents who knelt before him and kissed, not his hand, but a big fancy ring he wore on his finger.

Then he bent down to me and tousled my hair that Maman had so carefully arranged earlier that morning.

"Et qui est çe petit bonhomme?" he asked. (And who is this little man?)

Maman was apparently in a coma from being recognised by name by this distant cousin, Bishop Martin Lajeunesse, so it was up to Doc to identify me.

"C'est notre plus jeune garçon, Germain, Monseigneur." he replied. (It is our youngest boy, Germain, my lord.)

It took me a minute to realise he was actually talking about me as I was seldom called by my real name, Germain. (I was so named by Doc after my paternal great-grandfather. I hated that name at first because it sounded feminine in English and was subject of my being teased as a "German" during the war years. As a result I tolerated being called baby until my teens)

Interior of Eglise Saint Jean Baptiste as it would be arranged for the Bishop's visit. From Capitale d'une Solitude by Germain Lesage OMI, 1946.

At last the Bishop entered the church. Maman came out of her paralysis and we followed.

I was really quite impressed by the ceremony that the Bishop officiated. The beanie on his head had been replaced by a fancy high pointed hat with big ribbons hanging out the back. He wore white gloves and held in his hand a long gold pole that was curled at the top.

The inside of the church fairly dripped with decorations of flags and flowers. Yes, there were Maman's glads in front of the altar! Maman's cousin, the Bishop, had a beautiful singing voice that even Pé'Père couldn't match so the choir seemed to try extra hard to sound nice.

Finally the reason for His Excellency's

coming was revealed as some older boys and girls went up to the fence and the Bishop gave them each a gentle pat on the face and, calling them by name, made a sign of the cross with his thumb on each forehead. The boys all wore clean white shirts and the girls, frilly white dresses and bonnets. It really was something and, for once, I kept close watch on everything that was going on, anxious to find out what it was all about.

Near the end, this great visitor faced us and, holding his golden pole with one gloved hand and waving the other hand at all of us, it was over and we all began to leave. But there was to be no crêpe brunch that day, for we were all invited to an outdoor feast. The missionary Brothers had set up a number of rough lumber tables in front of the convent, and we helped ourselves to baked whitefish and moose meat stew with bannock or buns aplenty and all kinds of fancy deserts to choose from. Obviously Maman's cousin was no ordinary black robe to merit such a banquet. The nuns and kitchen staff in white aprons moved among the tables, passing out mashed potatoes or turnips and other more tasty things.

At last, it was ending and with much more ring kissing, the bishop made his way back to his aeroplane and took off with a roar. Maman stood on the shore waving her white handkerchief goodbye, at times stopping to use the hankie to wipe away tears of joy.

While she waved away, Doc went into his hospital office to open the package that His Excellency had surreptitiously slipped him while Maman wasn't watching. I noticed that it made a gurgling sound as he walked. Could it be birch syrup?

Needless to say, the whole gala event made quite an impression on me and added confusion to my career choices of either cowboy or doctor. What would it be like to become a monseigneur and wear a big ring on my finger and all kinds of fancy garments?

Finally, I got up the nerve to ask Doc how one went about becoming a bishop. I was more than a little disappointed when he explained that first I would have to become a priest, that is, an ordinary blackrobe, and study for many years and if I was a really, really good priest, the Pope might choose me to wear the purple beanie.

But what do priests do, I wondered, besides talk for so long in church and recite magic words like "Dominus vobiscum!"?

Doc did his best to explain the priestly calling by telling me the story of those two priests who long ago, in 1846, had come to Ile a la Crosse to tell the native people about God and God's special son, Jesus. He spoke of these two missionaries' hard life in a strange land, of their work to build the school and the hospital so that these people would be well both in soul and body.

I   soon   lost interest. Darned if I was going to go through all that just for a fancy ring and a pointed hat!

CHAPTER 7- THE TRAVELLING MEDICINE MAN

"Muskox Operation" Every Winter For Dr. P. E. Lavoie in Far North

NORTH BATTLEFORD.—Dr. P. E. Lavoie, Saskatchewan's most northerly doctor, reaches for a map when news folk ask him about his territory. It spans the Province for the western boundary to the third meridian, and sprawls northward from Ile a la Cross clear through to the 59th Parallel. Medical officer for approximately 1,200 Indians who dwell in those regions, and provincial health official responsible for the welfare of the indigents among the remaining 1,200 citizens of far northern Saskatchewan he uses trucks, canoes and airplanes for travelling.

Once a month he takes a plane trip, 100 miles by air, to Portage la Loche where the Order of Grey Nuns operates a small dispensary and a four-bed emergency hospital to meet the needs of this isolated settlement. When emergencies arise, he visits the settlement more frequently. He chuckled when he related to the Star-Phoenix how "rush calls" from Portage la Loche are put through to him at Ile a la Crosse. The message is sent by wireless from the Hudson's Bay post to Fort McMurray. From there it is dispatched by wire to Edmonton, and relayed in turn, to Saskatoon, Meadow Lake, and Ile a la Crosse. "It usually gets through in two hours," he grinned cheerfully.

Doctor Lavoie believes that nowhere in Canada are the benefits of family allowances more to be seen than in the once indigent and still isolated areas of northern Saskatchewan. He is especially impressed with the wisdom of having the mothers handle the allowances. He mentioned several settlements he has visited recently where he noted that the ragged and skimpy clothing that had done duty for winter wear for the children in previous years, had been discarded for cosy ski suits, bought from the family allowance cheques. Better clothing and food, and education in the principles of healthful living are having a beneficial effect, he declared, adding that health conditions generally in the north are showing a marked improvement.

In his first visit "outside" for five years, Doctor Lavoie visited Regina recently. Returning through here, en route to his base at Ile a la Crosse, he was in a hurry to answer a call to investigate health conditions, especially among children, at far northern Camsell Portage, on the eastern reaches of Lake Athabaska.

TOUGH JOURNEY

He was looking forward, as only one who is 100 per cent sold on his job could do, to the journey that to this department looked like a one-man Muskox operation. It meant a night bus trip to Meadow Lake, catching the first fish truck out of the thriving town, bound for Ile a la Crosse; bucking unpredictible winter roads, winds and weather through endless miles of unsettled territory to the northern outlet of the Beaver River; a brief halt at Ile a la Crosse to check things, and to prepare for a flight over the desolate northern hinterland territory to his objective, not far from the 59th parallel, where a mere handful of Saskatchewan citizens are in dire need of medical advice.

His official duties done for the day, or week, Doctor Lavoie asks for nothing better than to relax in his home near the Ile a la Crosse mission, where he can pursue his favorite hobby, delving into the early records of the historical region that surrounds him.

He knows the story as few others do.

Farewell Party for Grain Buyer, Wife

ADANAC.—A farewell party for Mr. and Mrs. Imrie was held Friday

TLU EPIDEMIC

55

The newspaper story illustrates some of the special conditions that working in the North imposed on Doc. In this cell phone age, it may be difficult for people to grasp the continual challenges facing a medical doctor doing his best to look after the health of a small population spread out over a vast expanse of uninhabited wilderness.

Distance was the hardest factor to overcome. Doc spent as much time travelling from place to place as he did actually providing treatment. Most of this travel was affected by a climate that could be harsh, even dangerous at times.

A winter blizzard might be life threatening whether you were behind a team of sled dogs or in an aeroplane in which the instruments might be limited to a compass. A forced landing site might be no more than a small lake or slough surrounded by tall spruce or poplar.

A summer windstorm might strand a water traveller for several days on a bleak shoreline where the possibility of seeing another human being would be next to nil.

One suffered frostbite in winter and bugbites in summer.

Doc walking up from the aircraft at the dock to the waiting northern taxi, a horse and wagon.

Even when you had reached your destination, there was not likely to be a comfortable hotel to stay in, nor a restaurant to eat at. One had to depend on the kindness and welcome of the residents of the particular hamlet. It might be a place on the floor for your bedroll and perhaps a dish of beavertail stew in a tin bowl for supper and some dried fish and tea for breakfast but they shared what they had at hand. Many times Doc thanked God for the open generosity of northern people. Without it, his job would have been well nigh impossible at times.

As explained in detail later, the northern traveller was often totally immobilised during the seasonal changes of freeze-up and break-up of the waterways. Doc

did have to take chances at times in
these between season's travelling on unsafe
ice to attend to an emergency medical case.
He put his life in the hands of a trusted
native guide in those instances.

At times, -40 degree temperatures forced
an emergency rest stop to build a spruce
bough shelter and a fire. Even the aeroplane
froze up at those temperatures and
challenged the bush pilot to find a safe
place to land and light his "fire-pots".

*It took several hours to get the aircraft
engine warm enough to turn in very cold
weather.*

There is one misplaced photograph that
Doc had which showed two M and C Airways
WACO biplanes on their noses on the ice
within several hundred meters of each other.
First one aircraft hit an ice heave off Big
Island when landing on Lac Ile-a-la-Crosse
resulting in an instant stop and nosedive of
the machine.

M and C responded to the downed pilot's radio call for help by sending a second WACO. Would you believe that this second plane hit the same ice heave with identical results? Fortunately neither pilot was seriously hurt but the rescue pilot took a long time recovering from the embarrassment.

One particular float landing scared the daylights out of Doc. George Greening was flying him to Camsell Portage in late October. As they descended for a landing, they saw the unmistakeable sheen of new ice on the lake in front of the village. There was no turning back as the WACO was very low on fuel. So George tried a trick he had heard of, which was to skim the ice at take-off speed several times with his floats to break up the new ice to create a long enough channel of open water on which they were able to land safely without damage. After gassing up at the M and C shack, he used the same broken ice channel to take off again when Doc had finished his call.

Doc was to describe the experience this way. "That damn George! He scared me so much I wanted to pray but I even forgot how to do it."

Doc's constant trips were a hardship for Maman who was left alone to look after the children while wondering if 'le docteur' would return safely to his hearth this time. This page from the Nov.Dec 1951 issue of 'Island Breezes' makes the point.

59

WHERE'S DOC ?

"Not at home very often" answers Mrs. Lavoie. It's not easy to keep tab on his many trips but here's what the reporter was able to muster: On Nov. 6, Doc paid a visit to Beauval. On the 14 he flew to Buffalo Narrows by special plane and returned on the schedule. A week later he was in LaLoche for the first time after freeze-up. He had to crowd all his business into an hour or so. Again to Beauval on the 25th, he continued to Meadow Lake for a "bug" check-up. A few days later he returned with Mrs. Lavoie who had visited her sister in P.A. Doc headed north To Buffalo Narrows on Dec. 3 and to Buffalo River the next day. This last trip was really one of mercy. Aged Mrs. Billette who longed to return home to die near her loved ones had been taken -- by snow-mobile and stretcher -- to the plane on three different occasions, and all in vain: It wasn't a question of "no place at the inn" but no space on the plane. Finally Dr. Lavoie's patience, kindliness and snowmobile brought Mrs. Billette home. Doc is now back. . but for how long ?

- - - - - - -

Men willingly believe what they wish. --Caesar

AMBULANCE PLANE

Four mercy flights were made during the past month. Shortly after freeze-up Mrs. Maxime Lemaigre was flown in with baby André who was suffering from severe burns. Later Mrs. Josephine Morin was taken in from Buffalo N. Mrs. Marie Julien was flown in from Cree Lake for a cast on her fractured arm. The last trip was on December 9 when Sister A. Houle was transported to St. Paul's Hospital in Saskatoon.

BABIES -- ALL GIRLS

Doubtless in view of the coming Leap Year, the birth register counts no boys on its pages this time: GIRLS were born to: Mrs. J.B. Maurice -- ELEONORE, on October 15; Mrs. V. Wolverine, ROSE, on Nov. 17; both are from Patuanak. Mrs. Archie Buffin -- DORIS, on Oct. 30; from Beauval. Mrs. Ambroise Lariviere -- JULIA, on Oct. 19; Mrs. P. Aubichon, SUZANNE, on Nov. 17; Mrs. Eugene McKay -- BEATRICE, on Nov. 24; Mrs. Melchior Bouvier --RoSE LINDA, on Nov . 28; Mrs. Jimmy Morin--DOROTHEE, Dec. 7; the last five are all from Ile a la Crosse.

- - - - - - - -

Wrinkles should merely indicate where smiles have been.
--Mark Twain

The 'bug' mentioned in the article was the twin track Bombardier Snowmobile the department had provided Doc to replace dog team travel in winter. Thankful for the comfort and warmth that this vehicle provided, Doc nevertheless remarked that at least the dog teams did not get stuck in slush or breakdown halfway from nowhere. As Doc was admittedly a duffer with mechanical things he regularly took René along as driver cum engineer on these Snow-bug trips.

On one occasion, coming back from a medical visit to La Loche, he gave a ride to several Grey Nuns going to Ile a la Crosse to visit their colleagues. Suddenly, the engine stopped. In the growing darkness and cold, René checked all the usual things, frozen gas line, broken fan belt, spark plugs and battery cables. He could find nothing wrong. Yet repeated tries failed to bring the vehicle to life and the interior temperature was dropping rapidly. It was a long way to the nearest shore where a fire might be made. The dear Sisters, meanwhile, had begun a rosary, fervently praying for a miracle.

René had almost decided to walk on to try and find help when, for some reason, Doc ran his hand under the dash. Just then the panel lights flashed on momentarily. Frantically, René searched for and found the loose wire that had become detached from the ignition. Soon, they were on their way again and getting warm. There isn't much traffic on these northern natural highways and perhaps it was truly a miracle that a serious tragedy was avoided in this instance.

In the mid 1930's, the provincial government decided to build a bush road from Green Lake to the south shore of Lac Ile-a-a-Crosse (Fort Black) as a make work project for people on relief. Not much better than a wagon road, nevertheless some truckers from Meadow Lake, the closest railway siding, decided to brave the new road. Sometimes the road was dry, though rough. Often it was two muddy ruts and even rougher.

Section of the bush road from Green Lake to Fort Black.

For example, on one occasion Norman Acton took three days to make the trip. Wally Walcer and I had hitched a ride with him coming home from boarding school for the summer holidays. It was just before the yearly Saint John the Baptist religious celebration, June 24th, in Ile a la Crosse and a number of Green Lakers got a ride on the load to take part in the feasting. Acton divided the passengers into two work parties. While one group pried and shoved the truck through one mud hole, the second group went on ahead on foot to cut trees to fill in the ruts with at the next bad spot. Wally and I were allowed to sleep in the cab after dark when the mosquitoes got fierce. Norman and the others slept on any dry spot they could find.

Having made it to Fort Black, we all had to offload the freight into a waiting scow to be taken to the village of Ile a la crosse and further North to other waiting villages. The best you could say about the system was that the freight costs were lower than air freight and was more frequent than the Big River scows or swing teams which only made it twice a year.

Barring extra heavy snow falls, using the road in winter was considerably easier, unless there was a mechanical breakdown. Equipped with snow ploughs, the trucks would take a chance travelling on the ice when the road ended. With the center portion of the 'Vee shaped' plough cut out to provide just two tracks for the wheels, the trucks could make it to Buffalo Narrows and Patuanak fairly quickly, compared to summer scow transport.

63

Of course, it was still the unforgiving
North and the trucker took his chances that
he would not break through the ice. One or
two trucks a year went to the bottom so the
driver and any passenger kept one hand on
the door handle at all times when on an ice
road.

"*Maybe it isn't safe to cross today!*"

The truck drivers became dashing heroes
in the northern villages, and arguments
often centered on who was the bravest; Henry
Schneider or Wilf Widmyer; Lee Brander or
Norman Acton?

Doc recalled one trip back from a visit
south riding with the Brander Brothers in
two trucks laden with beer for Buffalo
Narrows. Lee Brander took the lead with the
plough while Doc rode with Hugh Brander in
the second truck. Just as they were about to
get on the ice at Fort Black, Hugh warned

Doc to roll his window down and to partially open his door, just in case. Doc soon experienced the reason for these precautions. Hugh let his brother Lee get ahead about 400 meters before following.

When Doc recounted the adventure, he frankly stated that it was once when he soiled his 'long-johns'.

"I was looking ahead at Lee's truck and I saw the ice go down under his wheels and rise back up like it was jelly. I yelled at Hugh, 'He's going to break through! Stop!'"

"But Hugh just told me, 'Don't worry Doc. It's O.K. Maybe you should close your eyes until we get across.'"

"Well I tried to do that but my eyes just opened again and I felt forced to watch Lee's truck. So I pushed open my door some more ready to jump out. My Lord I was terrified. But we made it across to the mission and I went straight to the church to say thank you to God!"

Yes! Those 'modern advances' caused a lot more stress than riding in a toboggan or a canoe.

CHAPTER 8: - "MESTIGOSEW" AT PLAY

Being a kid in Ile-a-la-Crosse meant being almost totally free whenever school was out. Mind you, summer was always a little slow in coming but we rushed the season. It was the tradition of my native friends and me to go 'pakasimowin' on May 24th, "the queen's birthday! If we don't get a holiday we'll all run away!"

This first swim almost always was a trial because ice pans were sometimes floating still in the centre of the lake. But with Cree equivalent taunts of "chicken-shit" whipping us on, we'd dive in off the big government wharf and each one tried to be the last one out. This was usually Jean-Marie. Belying his feminine sounding name, he was tougher than the rest of us boys and seemed able to withstand the frigid water for a painfully long time. But I was never the first one out, thank God! "Chummy" had the ability to dive in and out in one almost unbroken motion. The rest of us soon followed, shivering uncontrollably. Unfortunately my 'pale-face' skin showed the bluish goose bumps clearly, which led to a lot of snickering by my browner friends.

By mid-June, when school was out, we would spend nearly all of our daylight hours in, or on, the lake. Skinny-dipping? Never! But we had no use for bathing suits. We simply took off our cotton shirts, tied the two sleeves around our waists, then pulled

the shirttail up between our legs and
rolled it over the knotted sleeves. Our
shirts were seldom dry, but they were always
clean.

Modest as this swimwear seemed to us, it
was too much for some of the missionaries. I
particularly remember old Frère Auguste
chasing us down the beach in front of the
residential school girls' playground yelling
at us in French about our nakedness. The
poor old brother never caught us fleet of
foot kids. He was too used to plodding after
his herd of cows, which he tended tenderly
for the mission. He could have used a dip in
the lake himself. How I remember the pungent
smell of manure whenever Maman forced us to
attend "la bénédiction" in the overly small
and overly heated girls residence chapel.
The good brother's malodorous presence was
almost enough to make you run out gasping
for breath before the first decade of the
rosary was finished.

But swimming wasn't our only activity. A
favourite was climbing the wooden water
tower, which provided the mission with
running water. We usually managed to get
halfway up before Père Rosignol would show
up threatening us with eternal damnation if
we didn't come down "toute suite"! Frankly,
I was secretly relieved when he showed up
because I always felt the onset of vertigo
about 20 feet up, and my fear of chickening
out was greater than my fear of heights.
Once, when he didn't show up, I was lucky
enough to get a giant sliver in my inner

thigh from one of the log beams. It required medical assistance to remove, and Doc threatened me with cutting off my "pissette" if I ever climbed the tower again. This was apparently sufficiently face saving to impress my friends and I've always felt grateful to Doc for giving me this "out".

Note: The lower part of the hospital's wooden water tower. I can't say for sure if that's me or my older brother Emile.

The best indication that winter was ending was the game of "la pelotte", a game played with a sponge rubber ball and a "bat" that was usually just a handy stick about three feet long. There were 'teams' sort of. A pitcher and catcher were chosen but the resemblance to baseball nearly ended there. The pitcher had to loft the ball gently to the batter who could let as many strikes go by as his teamates' patience allowed. If the batter swung and missed he or she was out if the catcher caught the ball behind the plate in the air or after one bounce.

68

If the batter got a hit, he or she would start around first base and second base, -there was no third-, and managed to get back to home plate without being "hit" he/she was still 'alive'. Any one of the opposing team could put the base runner out by the simple expedient of hitting the runner with the ball between the bases. The fact that the ball was harder than it looked and stung sharply when it smacked into flesh gave added impetus for staying alive.

But if you should hit a fly ball and it was caught in the air out in the field that was disastrous for your team. In that unfortunate event, the whole team was out and had to take the field. Otherwise, your team went down one by one on "strike-outs", hit between bases, or flies caught on one bounce. If, however, a hitter hit a real long ball, or one that got lost in the weeds or brush, the batter could go around the bases extra times and each time he (seldom she) made the circuit before the ball was retrieved meant that an 'out' was back 'alive' again.

With a couple of good hitters a team could stay at bat forever, for that, and not the number of runs scored, was the object of the game. On a June 21st, the longest day of the year, my mother dragged me off the field of battle in still daylight at ten o'clock at night.

Another favourite pastime was playing "cowboys and Indians". It didn't seem

peculiar to me that my native friends all
wanted to be cowboys just as much as I did
because nobody wanted to be an Indian
because, you know, the Indians always lost.
So we had to do a lot of 'eenie meenies' to
choose the cowboys fairly. That was the only
fair part, at first, because the Indians
always had to pretend to shoot you with a
pretend bow and arrow while the cowboys
merely had to point their fingers and go
bang! and another 'injun' bit the dust.
Chummy was unkillable as an Indian though
because you could catch him, sit on him, put
your index finger in his ear and go bang
and, unfailingly, he'd bounce up yelling
"you missed me" or "you can't always hit".

In time, when the mission began to bring
in some silent movies, including some "Tom
Mix's", we discovered that those "dang
murderin' sheep herders 'ill eagly' sold the
injuns guns and whiskey." From then on, the
selected Indians were on a more even footing
with the cowboys, claiming that they, too,
had got guns from the bad white men.

CHAPTER 9: - GETTING EDUCATED

Almost from the moment that the Roman Catholic missionaries arrived at Fort Ile a la Crosse in 1846, they bent much of their efforts towards educating the local children. The native kids were taught to read and write, primarily in French at first, so that they could understand the tenets of the Catholic faith and recite the standard prayers correctly in both French and Latin.

This early effort to educate was soon expanded to a form of residential school so that the children from other northern villages could be brought in for schooling and Christianising. By my day, the late thirties and early forties, the Ile a la Crosse residential school had over a hundred boarding students. At some point, when the school was partially funded by government, the school had to switch to English as the language of instruction.

The village kids were taught as 'day scholars' for some years. But, perhaps fearing that they might somehow corrupt the residential kids with their worldly wise knowledge and habits, the mission eventually established a separate multi-grade classroom for the village children. Doc had other ideas about the education of his children, however.

When I was five years old, Doc decided that he wanted me educated in French along

with my older brothers; therefore I was to accompany Emile to the Jardin de l'Enfance residential school in Gravelbourg, the quasi-centre of French speaking Southern Saskatchewan. My eldest brother, René, had by then graduated to the Collège Mathieu, also located in bone dry Gravelbourg.

Rene and Emile waiting to fly South to Prince Albert where they went by train and bus to Gravelbourg Saskatchewan.

My memories of this experience are mercifully dim. I know that I hated it and spent a lot of time living up to my nickname, Bébé, by ceaseless crying. Then there occurred a painful event that turned out to be a blessing disguised as blood.

It was near the end of that first terrible school year. On a particularly hot day in early June, after a noon lunch of very salty soup, the children were sent outside to play, as usual, until the class bell rang. The salty soup, the dusty yard, the heat of the noon-day sun had driven me almost mad with thirst by the time the bell rang.

There was a strict rule that when that bell rang, the students were to go directly up to their classrooms, not stopping for any reason on the way.

But my thirst had made me rash. I ran into the playroom where the drinking fountain was. I was greedily gulping a mouthful of water when I got a blow on the back of the head that sent my forehead banging into the fountain.

Dazed, I hardly heard the tirade of the young nun who had caught me in my crime. Only when she noticed the blood dripping down my face did the scolding stop.

It wasn't long before Doctor Trudel, an old friend of Doc's, was sewing five stitches into my throbbing forehead. Nor was it long before the story got to my brother, René, at Collège Mathieu and he passed it on by mail to Doc and Maman.

With Maman crying, "Mon pauvre Bébé!" Doc caught the mail plane south and soon was pounding at the boarding school door. A brief visit with his friend, Doctor Trudel, had confirmed René's story. In no time flat, Emile and I had gathered our belongings and we were on our way home to Ile a la Crosse with Doc. René stayed on at Collège Mathieu to become the only boy in the family with a partial classical "Bac' des Arts" in French.

As for Emile and I, in the face of Maman's adamant refusal to even consider sending her two youngest to another boarding School, whether French or Swahili, Doc finally agreed to allow us to attend the local school and to be taught in English. He did so only on the understanding that we two would get a couple of hours a week of French vocabulary and grammar which the Grey Nuns, all French speaking, gladly agreed to provide.

I fell in love with my first teacher in Ile a la Crosse, Sister Brady. Under her gentle tutelage I learned to read and write in two languages. I even learned to do some arithmetic though it wasn't my best subject. At blackboard competitions, Lena Ahenakew could always beat me hands down in getting the answer to any Math problems.

What I loved best was reading. Every month, the Department of Education would send us a metal ammunition box full of books. It was my habit to start at one end of the box and read right through to the other end. If a book was particularly interesting, Sister Brady would allow me to take it home to finish. As Doc was also an avid reader, the two of us spent many a winter evening in front of our stone fireplace quietly reading. If I got stuck on a word, Doc would help me sound it out and then explain its meaning.

Doc had subscribed to every book club and magazine, both French and English, available back then. Whenever he found a passage that was   particularly funny or interesting, he'd say,

"Viens lire ça pour moi. "

Dutifully I would struggle through the text he indicated with occasional prodding from him. As a result I quite often got hooked on one of his books. So Doc's private bookshelf supplemented the children's books in the ammunition box with some quite adult reading. These stories occasionally made Sister Brady blush when I would tell her about them. But she never discouraged me from reading whatever drew my attention.

The mail-plane also made a weekly delivery of Doc's various newspapers. I became addicted to the comic strips in the Winnipeg Free Press and the Saskatoon Star Phoenix but I always had to wait patiently until Doc was finished reading the news before I got my turn at the papers. Sometimes, he would insist that I read a particular article before giving me the comic page. As a result I learned all about the Royal visit to Canada and of the atrocities of Hitler prior to and during World War II. Only after this directed reading could I satisfy my desire to catch up on the latest exploits of the Katzenjammer Kids and Mutt and Jeff. Even the pictures in the French Language newspapers like La Liberté et le Patriote broadened my view of the world outside of my little home village of Ile a la Crosse.

During these reading bouts,Maman,who didn't care much for reading in any language, except for her prayer book, would sit with her embroidery, emitting an occasional sigh of longing for civilised fellowship.

My brother, Emile, being older and less given to reading for pleasure, usually spent these evenings outside playing with the boys and girls of his age no matter how inclement the weather.

Quite often, when Maman would decree that it was bedtime, an argument would ensue if I was caught up in reading something particularly interesting. A couple of times, after Emile had gone to sleep in the bed we shared, Maman caught me reading with the help of a flashlight under the covers.

I was the first kid in Ile a la Crosse burdened with having to wear glasses.

CHAPTER 10:-ENTERTAINMENT? OH YES!

Besides reading, a favourite pastime was listening to the radio, still quite a novelty in those late thirties and early forties. Doc had bought a huge radio set, absolutely jammed with hot, glowing tubes inside a rounded wooden cabinet some three feet wide and four feet high. Size didn't guarantee reception, however, and we all got to be adept at slowly twiddling the knobs until "this is CBK Watrous in Saskatchewan" could be heard reasonably clearly.

The big Marconi ran on wet cell batteries that had to be re-charged regularly. For this purpose, Doc had had a "wind-charger" erected in the back yard. This contraption consisted of a two bladed propeller hooked up to a generator atop a 30 foot pole. A long fantail kept the prop constantly facing the wind which blew fairly regularly from the West across Rosser Bay.

Maman was terrified of the wind-charger from the first revolution. Perhaps the whirling propeller reminded her of her nightmare experience on her first aeroplane ride. She kept looking at it uneasily, and whenever the wind freshened and she could hear the generator atop the pole scream, she would kneel by her bed saying her rosary hoping the Blessed Virgin would talk her Son into once more calming the wind.

Doc would check the liquid battery with his rubber bulb gauge and if it was fully charged, he would go out and pull the control rope that disconnected the generator from the propeller which was left to free wheel at any speed it wanted. Wow! Did that thing whirr sometimes. But the high-pitched whine of the generator would stop.

The strongest winds maliciously seemed to blow whenever Doc was away. When that happened, Maman would run to the hospital hoping to find someone brave enough to shut down the screaming apparatus. Usually one of the missionary brothers would be called who would eventually come and give the control rope a tug. Emile would try to convince Maman that he could shut the generator off but she would not hear of it, convinced that her son might die if he were to do something wrong in the attempt.

Fortunately, before she could get up the courage to demand that Doc take the thing down, Maman got hooked on a radio soap opera. Every weekday, at two o'clock in the afternoon, you would hear the radio solemnly intone, "Un homme et son péché! Une autre des belles histoires des pays d'en haut". (Translated, "A man and his sin! Another beautiful story of the upper country".)

The main character was a fellow called

Seraphin Boudrier, and his sin was that he was a miser, squeezing every penny till it hurt. Despite his hidden cache of cash, his poor wife suffered in abject poverty and shame while her husband wheeled and dealed everyone he could out of their money. Often, Maman would break into tears as Madame Boudrier suffered yet another humiliation at the hands of her husband. I suspect that Maman considered herself a kindred sufferer.

We two boys also had our favourite radio shows. We hardly ever missed Jack Benny's cheerful "Jello everyone!" We sat breathlessly through each episode of "The Shadow" and laughed at "Fibber Magee and Molly". We even tolerated Cecil B. DeMille's "Lux Theatre".

Almost religiously, every Saturday night, right after our weekly bath, we would huddle by the speaker to listen intently as Foster Hewitt described "Hockey Night in Canada". Even Doc would put down whatever he was reading to listen if "Les Canadiens de Montréal" were playing.

But Doc mainly listened to the news. Throughout the Second World War, he would catch every newscast he could, often with a map of Europe opened in front of him. We dared not make a sound during those news programs. He could freeze us in place with one baleful look if we breathed too noisily.

Occasionally, something in the system would break down and we were like addicts without a fix. If it was just a burned out tube, no problem. Doc always kept a whole set of spare radio tubes on hand. But if it was the wind-charger and the batteries failed to charge, things were more serious. Then it was that we had to call on George Ramsey who, because he could climb anything to any height without fear, bore the Cree nickname of "Anakwatchas" meaning squirrel. With just a rope tied around him and the pole, he would shinny up to the wind-charger in a minute where he would detach the generator and bring it down. Then Vic Marquis, the local Jack of all trades, would examine it and fix it.

Once fixed, the "Squirrel" would take the generator back up the pole to remount it. Usually, after an hour or so of reasonable wind, the battery was charged enough to put us back on the receiving end of CBK Watrous.

Besides the radio, we could maybe even go to the movies for entertainment. Surprised? Well, someone had donated a silent movie projector to the Ile a la Crosse mission when everyone down south was switching to "talking pictures". The priests ordered in some silent movie reels by mail plane every week.

Those silent movies made Charlie Chaplin and Buster Keaton familiar figures as we sat crowded into the boys' residence basement, to be almost smoked out by movie's end because all adult men and women smoked "rollies" or the pipe. Old Mrs. Couronne always mixed kinikinik bark with her pipe tobacco as did many of the other elders, and the smoke was so acrid as to make your eyes water.

Couronne Maurice with her pipe

This made it harder to read the sub-titles out loud as we all did who had mastered this skill in school. It cost ten cents for an adult and a nickel for kids 14 and under to attend these movies. Since they kept the film until the next plane out, a good pot-boiler, without too much of the female star showing, might be shown three or four times by the missionary Brother and us kids always managed to scratch up the five pennies to attend each extra showing.

Eventually, the village organised a recreation club and built a community hall where they could hold dances. This was in defiance of the fact that dancing was viewed as an occasion of sin by the mission authorities.

The organisers were going to pay part of the construction costs by showing movies, not just the silent movies, but "talkies". By that time the depression was about over and we were expected to pay 25 cents for

kids and 50 cents for adults to attend. To
show these movies, the villagers had to set
up a power plant as only the mission had
electricity then. The electrical engineer
cum movie projectionist was Vic Marquis, a
shell-shocked survivor of the Great War, who
had a magical ability to fix things that
broke down.

And break down they often did, usually
just as the hero was about to jump off his
horse onto the runaway team thus saving the
"purty school-marm". The screen would go
brown as the galloping music slowed to a
growl. If it was the power plant, Vic would
be heard cursing when repeated pulls of the
starting rope would only give us brief
glimpses of shadows on the screen and grunts
from the speaker box. Vic never gave up,
though, and eventually he would get whatever
had quit going again.

Meanwhile we would sit in the light of
cigarettes exchanging predictions of what
would happen next in the film. Some of the
older boys and girls exchanged more than
predictions. So, all in all, these equipment
failures were accepted with reasonably good
grace. Each film was shown on three nights
and most of us attended all three showings
and could recite the dialogue by heart by
mail plane day. It was a good way to improve
our English but it didn't help our reading
like the "silents" had done.

Dances were held in that community hall
on occasion. There was no pre-arrangement

for a dance band. Whoever had a violin
or guitar would bring it along. Everyone's
favourite on the violin was Auguste
Durocher. He could pick up a tune and play
it after hearing it only once. What's more,
he provided his own rhythm section by
drumming his moccassined feet inside a
wooden butter box. There was no door charge
but a silver collection was taken up
occasionally to reward the musicians.

Children were allowed to attend these
dances and many soon learned how to jig and
foxtrot. We delighted in watching the
intricate patterns of the square dances and
laughed heartily when the caller threw in a
few funny lines of his own.

Were we ever bored? Never!

CHAPTER 11:-IN THE STEPS OF THE MEDICINE MAN.

Since most of my friends were planning to become trappers and fishermen like their Dads, I felt obligated to follow in Doc's footsteps to become a man of medicine. The Cree title of "maskihkiwino" which translates simply as "medicine man" still invoked a particular connotation of shaman or wizard among the native people and as a result, this heathen term was sternly decried by the missionary priests.

But being a "docteur" like my father was apparently O.K. So, in slack times, I often hung around the hospital observing. The patients didn't mind, but little Soeur Gaudette, the matron, would eventually show me out before I got tiresome. Most of the sick men suffered from tuberculosis, I think, while most of the women suffered from being too fat which I later learned had something to do with having babies.

Doc's continuous battle against tuberculosis was slow and ponderous, like trench warfare. He also had regular skirmishes against various forms of Venereal Disease. Occasionally he had to remove infected tonsils and appendixes in remote hamlets without benefit of an antiseptic surgery.

Doc was never one to talk much about his medical triumphs. But these were what made

Maskihkiwino Lavoie a revered name throughout the North. Like the little girl whose cheek had been torn almost completely off by a swipe from a startled black bear. She had been picking saskatoon berries on one side of a bush while the bear was feeding on the other side. They apparently backed into each other. The big flap of flesh exposed much of her jaw and when she was brought in to Doc, he knew that even though he had no training in plastic surgery, he was forced to try his best to repair the damage. He did and people were amazed that not only did the little girl grow up to be a handsome woman, but her facial scar was almost imperceptible.

Then there was the teenager who was severely hurt in an accident while tobogganing down the banks of the Beaver River by Beauval. The toboggan was smashed to pieces when it hit a huge rock and a shard of wood some twelve inches long skewered him through the scrotum. Again Doc's surgical skills were challenged and he sewed the boy together again. In fact, in later years, the boy turned man was often heard to brag,

"That Doc he fixed me so good! People say I could never have kids. Well I got six kids and each one look different."

Doc became the recipient of a huge polar bear hide as a result of keeping an RCMP's badly broken arm from becoming part of an official report. The young constable had just been assigned to Ile a la Crosse after serving a stint in the Arctic. Unfortunately, as he was getting off the Stinson bush plane at the landing dock, he slipped on the wet float and in trying to catch his balance, hit his arm against the wing-strut and then fell heavily into the dock with his injured arm getting most of the weight.

When Doc got a look at the X-ray of the arm, he discovered a multiple fracture that he felt would warrant a fly out to a southern specialist. But the young Mounty begged Doc to try to fix the break himself and, if possible, to keep the injury secret as the Force, in those days, was not given to coddling cripples. Doc was touched by the young man's plight and after studying the X-ray again carefully, he decided to try his best to fix the break, and furthermore, to keep the injury out of his records.

The young constable's arm healed flawlessly and his career was protected. Out of gratitude, he insisted that Doc accept the undressed polar bear hide that he had brought out of Holman Island in the Arctic.

Typically, Doc refused any kind of payment for his ministration, but his grateful patient pressed further.

"Look Doc," he said "I am single and I have no place to keep anything this big and I can't even afford to get it mounted.

You'd be doing me a favour by taking it off my hands."

Finally Doc relented. It cost him $60.00 to have the skin properly mounted, a sum he could hardly afford himself in those depression days. But as far as us kids were concerned, it was money well spent. About ten feet long from nose to tail and almost as wide, it lay on our living room floor in front of the big stone fireplace for nearly eighteen years. I spent many happy childhood hours stretched out in luxury on its length, sometimes wrapping myself completely in its warmth. We learned to avoid stepping barefoot on the bear feet out of respect for the three inch claws. I still have this magnificent trophy, somewhat tattered from its 60 years of hard use, but still a proud reminder, not only of Doc's skill, but of his warm-hearted care for the unfortunate.

Polar bear mounted nearly 60 years ago.

A final example of Doc's medical ability to adapt was the case of John the Swede's legs.

A tough Scandinavian trapper and fisherman called John Swanwick showed how highly Doc's medical skill was regarded. John had fallen through the ice on Clear Lake one particularly cold day. He had been running behind his dog team to keep warm when he fell through. The ice had formed a wide crack because of a temperature change. A thin layer of new ice had formed soon to be covered with enough snow to hide the danger. The dog team had gotten across, but John's greater weight crashed through. Instinctively, the trapper fell forward just as the ice gave way, but he got wet nearly up to the knees in the freezing water.

To make matters worse, frightened perhaps by John's involuntary yell as he fell through, the dog team took off like a shot dragging the cariole that contained the change of clothes and footwear which John now so desperately needed.

It was a good six or seven miles to the nearest shore where a camp fire might be made. John felt he might have a better chance of rescue if he headed straight for Buffalo Narrows. With his heavy aviator boots turned to blocks of ice around his feet, each step was harder and harder to take and soon he lost all feeling in his feet. Hours later, in the dead of night, he tumbled into his cold cabin. Quickly he

touched a match to the kindling in his
Quebec heater. It took some time before his
boots had thawed enough so he could take
them off. Finally he fell exhausted into his
bunk.

For the next few days, the tough Swede
would not face up to the tragedy that had
struck his feet. He tried massage with
liniment, hot soaks in the washtub. Finally,
when he saw the dead discoloured flesh
become worse, he gave in and asked his
closest neighbour to get word to the Doc.

Doc's immediate reaction was that both
legs would have to be amputated as soon as
possible because gangrene had begun to set
in. Unfortunately, the weather had soured so
that an aircraft wouldn't be able to fly the
patient out for several days. Doc explained
the situation to the stoic trapper.

"Vell Doc, if my legs got to be cut off,
you yust go ahead and do it yourself. By
yumping yimminy, I bet you can use a saw
better than those damn doctors down south
who never cut a stick of vood in their
lives. I put a new blade on my svede saw
yust a few veeks ago. You'll find it hanging
on the vood shed."

But Doc had just experienced travel in
the warmth and relative comfort of what came
to be called a "snow-bug" on his trip from
Ile-a-la-Crosse to Buffalo. Waite Fisheries
of Buffalo Narrows had recently acquired a
new-fangled twin track covered snow machine

built by a fledgling   Quebec company called
Bombardier.

*Eventually Doctor Lavoie was supplied with a
Bombardier "Snow -Bug" by medical authorities
to replace winter travel by dog team.*

If he had to do the double amputation
himself, Doc decided, he would rather do it
in the sanitary operating room of St. Joseph
hospital. Len Waite readily agreed to run
doctor and patient the 28 miles to Ile-a-la-
Crosse.

And so the double amputation was done,
and done successfully. It wasn't long before
the tough Swede was demanding to be let out
of his hospital bed. When Doc gently pointed
out that he would have to be fitted with
artificial legs before he could walk again,
John was adamant that he couldn't wait that
long.

"Doc, a 'Catlik' like you ought to know that a man's knees can hold him up! I still got my knees and a bit of leg left on each side. You yust took the stitches out. So here goes."

So saying, the trapper was out of bed and he hobbled along on his knees on the linoleum, to the consternation of Doc and Nurse Evangeline Russel.

"Wait a minute, John," Doc said. "At least let the nurse put some kind of stocking and some padding on you because your knees must hurt walking on them like that."

"Vell, you're right Doc. But you know what I really need is a pair of those pads that hockey players use."

Soon, John Swanwick was fitted with an old pair of René's hockey pads and it wasn't long before he was stumping along the hospital corridors, out the door and on his way into town. Eventually, Doc managed to have him fitted with a proper pair of prosthetic legs and stories abounded about John the Swede's ability to carry his canoe and gear across the roughest portage on his "store-bought" legs.

CHAPTER 12:-CHASING THE ELUSIVE BUCK

Back: René & DOC
Front: Emile & Bébé..

The Lavoie family lived reasonably well in Ile a la Crosse, not lacking or wanting for much. But then, we were never rich either. The following exchange of letters between Doc and the provincial department of health tells it best. The modern reader should know that it was annual, not monthly, salary under discussion.

Re typed from Doc's carbon.

Saint Joseph Hospital
Ile a la Crosse,

Feb 18,1936

Hon.Doctor Uhrich

Minister of Public Health,

Legislative Buildings,

Regina.

Dear Doctor Uhrich:

Although I do realize the difficulties of this hard time
and the financial worries of the government, allow me to ask for
a raise to my salary.

As you are aware my salary is paid jointly by the
Department of Indian Affairs and your department; $2000 from
Ottawa and $1600 from the province. As you may be aware that my
work amongst the people belonging to this province takes more of
my time than with the Indians, do you not think it would be only
fair to get $2000 as well from your department?

A salary of $3600 {per year}may look large to a citizen of
Regina, but here it is quite the contrary. The cost of living is
doubl he one of Regina. For instance a sack of flour paid $2.50
in the South cost here $5.00; butter 50 cents a pound, meat the
same. In summer fresh meat can only be got by plane at 7 cents a
pound freight. As for fresh fruit, we go without, unable to
afford it. Therefore a salary of $3600 has only the buying value
of $1800 only.

The transportation of my children outside for their
education costs me more than the tuition fees. So do you not
think it is reasonable for me to ask for a small raise of $400?
Besides I believe that I have saved more than that to the
government in keeping here for treatment all the serious cases
at the exception of two cases that in the past would be sent
outside at government cost.

Hoping that you will take my request in serious
consideration, I remain your obedient servant

P.E.Lavoie,MD Medical Superintendent

The official reply, as might be expected, was less than encouraging.

Deputy Minister of Public Health

Saskatchewan

Regina, February 28, 1936

P.E.Lavoie,Esq.,MD, Superitendent

Ile a la Crosse Hospital

Dear Doctor Lavoie:

I have your letter of February 3rd before me, as well as your letter of February 18th addressed to the Honourable J.W. Urich, MD.

As you will recall, when the arrangements were made for your appointment at Ile a la Crosse Hospital the salary decided upon was $3600 per annum, and as I have told you previously, the whole matter at the first of 1935 was taken out of our hands when the Government cut all salaries, including yours. What amounts may be obtained by this Department from the Federal Government has no bearing whatsoever on the total salary you receive, and while I realise that certain commodities must of necessity be very high in that area, I think you will agree that there are many other overhead expenses in the more developed communities which neutralithe high cost of food supplies at Ile a la Crosse. I therefore feel that the salary you are getting is proportionately much higher than a somewhat higher scale would be in the city of Regina. …etc…

Yours very truly,

R.O. Davidson,MD

Deputy Minister

Despite the hard reality that neither government would ever pay him what might be expected to be a medical doctor's income, even when war effectively ended the depression, Doc opted to stay on in the north. Why? Certainly it was not because Maman was urging him to stay in Ile-a-la-Crosse. On the contrary, she never accepted life in this isolated place as being a permanent reality.

It must have had something to do with the satisfaction Doc got from his service to northern people of whom he became genuinely fond. He admitted that the only thing that bothered him about practicing medicine in the north was that there was not another doctor to provide that "second opinion" whenever he was unsure about a diagnosis.

But, it must have bothered him sometimes to read of his colleagues in the south, like Doctors Trudel and Souci, who profited from the upturn in the Saskatchewan economy to become very well off.

Perhaps it was hearing about Doctor Souci's investment in a successful cattle ranch that prompted Doc to get into the mink ranch business. Whatever the reason, it was a big mistake.

Halvor Ausland had established the first mink ranch in our area. He liked to brag that he made more money in one year of ranching than he had made in ten years of trapping and fishing. With game fur becoming more and more scarce in most northern fur blocks, the canny Norwegian preached that you would make more money from fish by using it as mink feed than by selling it to the fish buyers. The evident success of his Deep River Fur Farm seemed to prove him right.

Doc got hooked on this story of easy riches fairly early on and he bought a small breeding stock from Ausland which was kept in individual pens behind our shed on the mission grounds. Suddenly, fishing off the government dock became, for us boys, a job instead of a pleasant pastime and, as such, it became tedious. Doc had to resort to offering each young fisher ten cents a fish to feed his mink.

During the winter, he had to buy fish from the commercial fishers to keep his stock alive until spring. When the first batch of baby minks were born Doc had to face the fact that he could no longer keep his minks behind our shed. But where to move them?

The answer came as a result of Doc's favourite hobby during his northern service, archaeology. He delighted in researching and locating old trading post sites, digging up many artefacts, most of which he donated to the RCMP Museum in Regina, including a complete set of copper tea pails from the two man size to the twelve man models.

During one of his archaeological explorations, Doc had discovered the site of old Fort Black that had been established by Alexander McKenzie as an XY fur trading post on the south shore of Lac Ile-a-la-Crosse in 1800. The builder and only manager of that XY post was Samuel Black, hence the name.

For a brief period the Fort Black post was in competition with both the Northwest Company and the Hudson's Bay Company posts built further up the lake.

and the beginning of the rival Central... by the North West Co.,the Hudson's Bay Co., and the XY Co. at Ile a la Crosse Saskatchewan.By Dr. L.L.Lavoie Medical Superintendent of Ile a la Crosse Hospital.

Fort Black

It is known in the history that some dissenting share holders of the North West Co. formed a Company known as the XY Co.Samuel Black came in to Ile A la Crosse for the XY, and built a rival post against the North West Co. Samuel Black was in charge of the post from 1800 to 1804.After the union of the Companies about 1805, he took charge of the N.W.Post on the lake. So all that is known by the history is that the XY Co. had a post at Ile a la Crosse; but Where? The tradition of the native population transmitted from father to son comes in for an explanation.

On the S.W. of township 74, range 12 there lies a promontary which closes in South Bay, and is the eastern shore of the lake.Beaver River is east of that land.That promontory is called Fort Black by the natives. If one asks to the natives on what grounds it is called Fort Black; invariably they all answer that it was there that the North West Co. was established long ago,(Kayas in

Cree:i.e.long long ago.) About the name of Black, nothing
is known.In face of this contradiction of the history, my
contention is that the Natives Contempories of Sam. Black
seeing him after four years of his establishment work for the
N.W.Co.were under the impression that he has been all the
time employed by this last company.Of an earlier origin
here of the N.W.Co. they are absolutely ignorant.
There are quite extensive remains on that point even today
and one is forced to conclude that it was quite a large
establishment.In fact they are the best preserved ruins in the
district, for the fact that this part has never been inha-
bited.The Natives have a superstitious fear of the place,
and the couple families who try to dwell there had to leave
after a short stay, claiming that ghosts were roaming in the
vicinity of that old fort.Knowing the dissolute and loose

Eventually the Fort Black post was abandoned when all three amalgamated under the HBC banner. Intrigued by the mention of a third post on the lake, Doc found evidence of cellars, stone chimneys, even a small graveyard indicating where the old fort had stood.

As the discoverer, Doc asked for a lease near the Fort Black site so that he could protect it from depredation. He was granted the lease and consequently, the Fort Black Fur Farm had a home.

Doc went into debt to keep the operation

going until the stock of mink was large enough to permit some pelting and, thus, some revenue. On the advice of Ausland he hired Tony Swensen to run the mink ranch for him. Doc imported some prize breeding males and bought some more pens which put him still more deeply in debt.

At about this time, my oldest brother, René, had enough of Collège Mathieu in Gravelbourg and decided that he would try his hand at mink ranching. As Tony's helper he learned the rudiments quickly and soon knew how to set fish nets summer and winter, how to grind the fish and mix it with a special mink meal essential to a healthy mink's diet.

Ausland had left out some details of mink ranching overhead. Imported mink stock, boats, fish nets, grinders and mixers, more pens, mink meal by the bag; all this on top of wages for two men put Doc ever more deeply in the red.

*Pictures of minks in pens and of
employees. White minks were in great
demand for the coronation of Elizabeth II.*

Then, one morning, René saw flames
shooting up from Tony Swenson's caboose.
When he got there, it was too late to do
anything but watch Tony's funeral pyre. The
RCMP investigation found that the poor man
had used a can of gasoline to light his
stove, and the explosion and fire that
resulted had killed him.

So René was left to look after the ranch
pretty well by himself. But not for long
because my other brother, Emile, saw this
sorry state of things as the ready excuse he
needed to also quit his boarding high school
in Regina so he could help his older brother
and save Doc's mink ranch from going under.
The two of them worked very hard for about

two years, but poor returns discouraged them so much that first one, then the other quit.

René took a summer job with Waite Fisheries of Buffalo Narrows running one of Waite's big fish buying boats on all the big lakes in our area.

Emile followed one of the Ausland boys to Big River where he became a taxi driver.

Doc had to sell off his stock to redeem some of his losses.

Eventually Emile, tired of being on call at all hours driving drunks home, returned to Fort Black and with help from other mink ranchers tried to re-establish some sort of mink operation. René too returned when Waite's fish buying boats were beached for the winter and he was out of work. When René fell in love and married teacher Thérèse Lepage, Doc gladly turned over the ranch to the two boys, happy to be out of it.

So Doc never got to be financially rich. He had to be satisfied to live on the meagre salary raises the two levels of government begrudgingly paid him. He had to accept that he was no business man like his friend Doctor Souci.

Emile became the unofficial boss of the ranch operation and with Thérèse keeping books, he managed to get the ranch on a profitable basis during the period when René and Therese had three children.

Eventually, as more and more mink ranches were established in the area, fish stocks became so depleted that my brothers decided to move the Fort Black Fur Farm, lock, stock and grinder to the British Columbia coast.

That Emile showed such business acumen doesn't surprise me, thinking back. After all, it was he who showed me that being the first kids in the village to get new bicycles, we had a glorious opportunity to make a little bit of cash. We offered bike rides to all comers for ten cents for kids, two bits for adults. We were

Our new bikes! Rental business at 10 to 25 cents a ride was good but resulted in a lot of breakdowns.

soon rolling in dimes and quarters but our bikes had to be constantly repaired, the village trail being very rough and the riders quite inept.

We made even more money from another of Emile's ideas. That was in the summer of 1946, the year Ile a la Crosse celebrated the centennial of the establishment of La Mission Saint Jean-Baptiste. The event brought hundreds of people from all over the North and many from the rest of Canada.

Canoe parking was at a premium and tents blossomed everywhere.

Parking spaces for canoes were at a premium during the 1946 centennial celebrations.

A Prince Albert entrepreneur made a mint by setting up a small railroad ride that kids who had fifteen cents, (two rides for a quarter) could board. Emile and I soon used up our cash reserves on the little train, a real novelty to anyone who had never even seen a real train except in movies.

This Toonerville trolley was kept busy at Ile a la Crosse giving rides to youngsters, most of whom had never seen a train or had a ride in a mechanical vehicle. It is believed the first of its kind to operate in the north. —Star-Phoenix Staff Photos.

The train ride was a big draw for both children and adults.

It happened that the July week of the centennial celebration suffered a rare northern heat wave. The heat drove Emile and me into the house often for a cold drink from the ice box. That's when Emile got the idea for a drink stand. Maman's 20 gallon wine crock was pressed into use. We filled it with water from the tap, and set it outside. We went to the ice house and hosed off the sawdust from a block of ice which we added in chunks to the water. Believe it or not, many were willing to pay a nickel for a small dipperful of ice cold water.

But Emile wasn't satisfied and insisted on expanding the business. Jumping on his bike, he rode off to the Bay to buy out their entire stock of "cool aid" type drink powders. Mixing up the first batch, we discovered it wasn't too palatable without sugar so, without her knowing it, Maman's stock of canning sugar was surrendered to the thirsty horde. Doc noted our enterprise and, in the interest of sanitation, he suggested we set up the folding table from the shed and get a half dozen cups from the kitchen cupboard and a pan full of water to rinse them out in after each use. Pretty soon we were mobbed with customers and had to make more trips to the ice house and to the garden hose which we used to fill our buckets of water. Before we knew it our drink powders and Maman's sugar were gone. We bought some lemons and some sugar at Marion's store which ended up being the thinnest lemonade ever made. Emile was about to raid Maman's stock of canned raspberries for juice when Doc decided we had impoverished the centennial celebrants enough and told us to close up shop.

We couldn't believe our eyes when we added up our not entirely honest profits.

It wasn't long before Maman discovered that there wasn't a grain of sugar left in the house. We had to spend some of our money at the Bay to restore her to sweetness.

But like any successful business men, we spent the rest of the centennial celebrations spending money like drunken sailors.

105

Some of the people from all over the North who
attended the Centennial ceremonies held for the
Ile a la Crosse Roman Catholic Mission. (1846-
1946)

CHAPTER 13:-SEX EDUCATION, DOC'S WAY!

There was a caragana bush growing just under Doc's office window which became my favourite hide-away. As the window was usually open on nice summer days, I was privy to many an interesting doctor / patient conversation. One particular day I heard Doc remonstrating with a trapper about his annual brush with gonorhea.

"Every spring it is the same thing, Harry. You come off the trap line and you get a dose! Why you can't be more careful with your love life, for goodness sake?"

The answer, thinking back, was a classic.

"Well, Doc. You've got to understand. Every fall and winter I spend six months or more not seeing any women except the panty pit'chers in Eaton's catalogue. Well you gotta know that when I finally come out of the bush, I've got a gaddam hard-on so big, I don't have enough skin left over to close my mouth! So I go crazy, ready to jump the first woman that'll let me, and those easy kind almost always is dosed up."

Of course, most of trapper Harry's explanation for his illness went over my head as my English wasn't as highly developed as my French or my Cree at that age. The smattering of vocabulary I had picked up from Pat and Mike Kennelly wasn't up to much. (Slim and Dot Kennelly had a small trading post business in the village for a few years but couldn't compete with the Hudson Bay Co. and soon left with their two boys, broke and discouraged.) Although I had added to my English lexicon through the "talkies", I often had to depend on my older brother René for clarification. Even though René, at that time, still attended the French language boarding school in Gravelbourg, somehow he had picked up a pretty good facility in English.

So I asked him, "Qu'est ce que ça veux dire en anglais,'a dose'?" He looked a little non-plussed so I pressed on.

"Et puis, quoi c'est ça un 'hard-on'?"

At that, my brother ran into the house yelling, "Maman! Bébé dit des mots sales!"

I hadn't realised that the words in question were dirty, and I soon lost my faith in René as a translator.

Another time I was walking with Doc on the footpath through the thicket of willows leading to the HBC store. Even at my young age, I knew of a lot of snickering that went on among the older boys and girls about the rabbit warren of trails that led into and out of "les saules". I had seen many a face turn red with the mere mention of this popular trysting place.

We hadn't yet left the willows when Doc and I were met by a pretty woman in her twenties. The scent of her strong perfume mixed with a natural sultriness was almost overpowering even for a kid like me. But Doc didn't seem affected except to say,

"Bellefille! You come to my office tomorrow morning for a shot and some pills and not any more boyfriends to visit you until I say it is all right."

The lady blushed, hung her head and walked on without a word. But I knew that she would obey her summons without question.

The incident left me wondering what the medical basis of the decree against boyfriends was. My sex education was rudimentary at best, and mostly wrong, at worst, at that time.

In my pre-school years I had once been asked by my little play-mate, Louise, to "play house". I wasn't sure how to play that game and when she explained it I wasn't sure I wanted to play.

"We are in the pretend kitchen," she said, "and we eat supper together. Then we wash the dishes and then we go to bed together because I'm the Mommy and you're the Daddy and then we have babies. See?"

Frankly, it sounded pretty dull to me and I only agreed to play if I could add a little excitement by having to fight off some bad guys who were always trying to get into our pretend house. So I ate the pretend supper with one hand and shot a few "baddies" with the other. I had to dispatch a couple more while we washed the pretend dishes. But it was when we had to go into the pretend bedroom to lie down in the tall grass, which was to be our pretend bed, that I felt most vulnerable. How was I supposed to keep an eye out for attackers, much less fight heroically for our lives, in that position, especially with Louise insisting on wrapping her arms around my neck so I could hardly breathe?

My introduction to sexual anatomy came some time later when Charlie Ramsey challenged me to yet another peeing contest. With our backs against the woodshed wall, we would unbutton our overall flies and "let fly" so to speak. I think I was about seven at the time while Charlie was at least nine. That gave him an advantage in size that I never quite overcame no matter how much water I had drunk prior to the meet. Besides, he seemed to have the ability to lengthen his equipment by virtue of a few preliminary strokes. Anyway, Charlie not only always won in peeing distance but then he would tease me that even one of his little sisters could beat me even though she didn't even have a"til'kolo"!

That taunt haunted me for some time. Was he saying that girls were made different from boys? How could that be? If they were denied the essentials, how could they relieve themselves?

I had to find out! I knew that I couldn't ask either of my older brothers without risking ridicule. Finally, timidly, I approached Doc, that fountain of knowledge about all things. It took Doc a while to catch the gist of my stammering question. When he did, he got up from his armchair and ordered me sternly to follow him.

"Vien-t-en avec moi!" he said.

Dutifully, I followed him out but I was scared spitless! Was Doc going to give me my first licking for broaching a taboo subject? My fear gave way to confusion as we crossed the wooden walkway to the hospital. Then we went down the longish hallway to his office where I was ordered to sit on the wooden chair by his desk. I sat in uneasy silence, breathing the aromatic scent of rubbing alcohol and strong soap mixed with a hint of iodine. Meanwhile Doc was studying his bookshelf, pulling out the occasional book and, after flipping through it, putting it back to try a different volume. Finally he settled on a particular tome and laid it open on his desk. With a half-smile on his face he sat down in his swivelled chair and faced me.

"Amène ta chaise içi a côté de moi."

As ordered, I moved my chair close to his from where I could see some drawings of human anatomy, two of them, in the open book. Doc explained that the one on the left was a male, and was careful to point out

where the penis hung   with the scrotum. He
indicated the red line leading to the
bladder, the urinary track. He went on to
explain briefly the function of the blue
line leading to the testicles. He told me
that I would understand that part better
when I was a little older.

Then he turned to the second figure, that
of the female, and pointed out the obvious
differences. No penis, no scrotum: just a
sort of a tunnel leading up to a balloon-
like area. There was a red line leading from
the bladder to... where?

"Mais comment font-elles peepee sans
"pissette?" I asked incredulously, still not
comprehending how girls could urinate with
that ridiculous set-up.

Doc was obviously restraining his urge to
laugh as he flipped a few more pages in the
book to reveal a photograph, full front
view, of a woman standing without a stitch
of clothes on.

My anatomy lesson continued until I sort
of understood the structure of the vagina
and why women usually had to sit or squat to
urinate.

So Charlie turned out to be only partly
right. Sure, girls lacked what boys had, but
there was no way that his sisters could beat
me in a peeing contest.

CHAPTER 14:-WALKING ON WATER

The lakes and rivers of Northern Saskatchewan were our roadways to the world. We floated on them in summer and tobogganed on them in the winter.

The Cree name for Lac Ile-a-la-Crosse was "Sakitawak" which roughly translated means "where the waters meet." Three rivers flow into the lake; the Canoe River from the West, the "Deep" River from the North and the Beaver River from the South. Only one river empties the lake, the Churchill River that meanders eastward from the extreme North end of the lake and continues on through a vast string of lakes and rapids before spilling at last into the salt water of Hudson's Bay.

Even the so called Deep River was really part of the Churchill waterway, and followed North to Lac La Loche and across the Methey Portage it linked up with the Lakes Athabasca and Great Slave and with the Mackenzie River to the Arctic Sea. No wonder that Ile-a-la-Crosse was an important centre of the fur trade from the mid 1700's to the late 1800's.

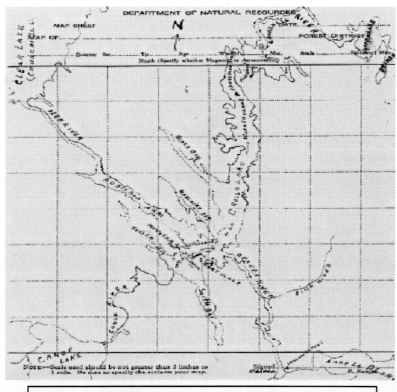

Doc's hand-drawn map of Lac Ile-a-la-Crosse.

As mentioned previously, there were two periods in the year when we were completely cut off from the rest of the world. One was the Fall freeze-up. The other was the Spring break-up. During those two "between seasons" even the bush plane was denied access to the northern outposts. Uncertain ice is a very unforgiving and undependable medium that can rip up floats or swallow up machines on skis.

The urge to go somewhere during those periods led to some real and some near tragedies.

The lakes always froze up first, the rivers remaining open longer due to the flow of water. Many a traveller ignored this fact to his peril. One of these was the missionary priest, Père Moreau.

Doc always said that Père Moreau trusted too much in God and not enough on common sense. This super energetic Pastor of the north-western Chipewyans deserves a book of his own.

One of the most famous stories about this priest was the time he walked on the water.

As Doc told it, Père Moreau had started out for Ile a la Crosse in a canvas covered freighter canoe from the Chipewyan village of Patuanak, a trip of some 30 miles down the north arm of the lake. Unfortunately for him and his three Indian companions, an early November frost had covered our area of Lac Ile-a-la-Crosse with a thin sheet of ice. This ice was too thin to walk on and too thick to break through without tearing the canvas cover of the canoe. The Beaver River's flow had left the lake open on the eastern side, and this permitted them to get to "La Grosse Ile", a big island in the main body of the lake.

They beached the canoe at the eastern sand point and walked the length of the island on foot to the western point from which they could see the village of Ile-a-la-Crosse almost a mile away across the expanse of new ice. As his three parishioners were discussing the wisdom of heading back to their canoe, hoping to get back home before the rest of the lake also froze over, the good Father dropped to his knees, spread out his arms cross-like and prayed for some time. Then he got up and beckoned his people to follow him across.

"God will protect you as He protected Saint Peter", he told them in the Dene language.

Timidly they followed his lead. They could see the ice bend beneath him but he did not break through. Neither did they and all four reached the mission safely to the consternation of those who saw them coming.

The next morning this early ice had vanished! A blessed miracle? Or just the luck of the foolhardy?

The day after the "miracle" when Père Moreau dropped in for his customary visit with Doc, I happened to be there. Usually the Reverend Father would list the symptoms of the mildly ill in his missions, and Doc would provide him with the medicines that were called for.

This time the good priest got a blast as well as his pills. Just the previous year, a young Hudson Bay Co. clerk had broken through the ice and drowned when he had attempted to skate down the Beaver River from Beauval, twenty miles to the South. Forcefully, Doc reminded the Missionary of that tragedy and how he and his three companions might easily have shared the same fate.

"Mais, Docteur, ne savez-vous pas que le Bon Jésu me tenait par la main en traversant?"

Doc threw up his hands in exasperation at this revelation that Jesus had held the Father's hand as he crossed.

Usually the ice was thick enough to walk on in early December and if the snow held off, the lake became an extended playground for us kids. Try as they might, the adults couldn't keep us off it before they thought it safe enough to play on.

Some of the kids had skates, including my brother Emile. One bright moonlit night early in winter, several of the older boys and girls challenged one another to a skating race across to Big Island. They were nearly there when Emile was forced to stop to re-tie his skate lace.

I had been left near shore by the mission dock. Suddenly, I saw the whole group skating back faster than I had ever seen any of them skate before, Emile leading the way. I could hear the girls screaming in terror. Out of breath, they all jumped up on the ice-bound mission wharf and the story came out brokenly as to what had happened.

It seems that as Emile was sitting on the ice to tie up his skate, the back tip of the blade broke through the ice. As the water bubbled up the small hole, Emile screamed a warning to the others and started skating back with his untied lace flapping. The sight of the puddle of water that appeared on the ice was enough to get everyone moving and with the moon now at their backs, they could see the ice making elastic "waves" behind Emile as he skated along. Rocket Richard himself might have had a hard time matching their speed that night.

When Emile had caught his breath and taken off his skates, he grabbed me by my parka hood.

"Not a word to Doc or Maman about this or you'll be sorry", I was told. I hated keeping secrets but I knew I had better keep this one.

Some of the kids, those without skates mostly, made small sleds about a foot wide and two feet long. The hand carved runners would be grooved with a knife to keep lengths of heavy quarter inch telegraph wire in place when the ends were nailed over on top of the runners' front and back. A few short boards nailed across held the sled together and provided the kneeling platform. Two short sticks with a be-headed nail stuck in the ends provided propulsion. You would

kneel on the little sled and pushing
with your sticks, ski-pole style, you could
achieve great speeds going across the bare
ice.

Jean-Marie had made a sled that was too
small for him, he said, and he gave it to
me. I soon became an adept "stick-sledder"
and hated it when too much snow on the ice
brought this fun to an end.

Doc had a theory about how Ile a la
Crosse had got its name and it had to do
with the way the lake would freeze first in
the currentless bays of the lake.

Other historians had insisted that when
Joseph Frobisher arrived at this lake in
1776 with his North West Company flotilla of
trading canoes, they saw some Indians
playing a game that resembled the Iroquois
game of la-crosse on an "island in the
lake". Most thought this was the "Grosse
Ile".

To Doc this Grosse Ile theory didn't make
sense as the only side of the big island
that might have permitted a game of any kind
was the open beach area on the south side of
the island. But this south side would have
been out of sight to the fur traders as they
entered the lake from the north on the
Churchill Arm.

The "ile" in question might have been the
isthmus itself on which the Fort Ile a la
Crosse originally was built. This might

easily have been mistaken as an island, being surrounded as it was on three sides by water. This possible game site made more sense as the finger of low lying land had been denuded of nearly all its trees by years of summer camps of the Woods Cree who needed firewood to cook and to dry their large catches of fish.

Doc's favourite explanation however was that what led Frobisher and his voyageurs to christen the place Ile a la Crosse was seeing a game resembling ice hockey being played there. From their written journals, he knew that the traders decided to winter there. When, in late Fall, the ice was already covering the quiet bays they noticed a number of young Indian men playing on the new ice. As the word "crosse" simply means "bent stick" in French, Doc could visualise this group of young braves batting a frozen moose dropping along the ice with the help of some crooked willow sticks. So there, Don Cherry!

As the ice thickened and became snow covered, most travel was by dog team. Even Doc would use this primitive conveyance when he visited villages less than a day's "mushing" away like Beauval, Buffalo Narrows, Canoe Lake and Patuanak.

Bush planes mastered the skill of landing on frozen lakes early on, but Doc's small budget had to be reserved for flights to his more distant patients. Even then his use of aircraft to visit his various villages might

120

be questioned by superiors in the
South who knew little of northern geography.
The following humorous exchange of letters
illustrates the point.

(Note: Retyped from the original)

DEPARTMENT OF NATIONAL HEALTH AND WELFARE

Qu'appelle Indian Hospital
Fort Qu'appell Sask.
July 3rd 1948

Dr. P.E.Lavoie
Ile a la Crosse Sask,

Dear Dr. Lavoie:

In the the Saskatchewan Government Airways account
for a trip made on April 14th and submitted under
Battleford Agency voucher #290, it is noticed single
fares were paid Ile a la Crosse to Patchanak while a
chartered tripwas made from Patghanak to Primrose Lake
and return and single fares again paid from Patchanak.
Iwas wondering why the plane was not chartered direct
from Primrose Lake and return, which would be most
economical.

(signed)
Regional Superintendent for
the Province of Saskatchewan.

Doc's reply has the tone of tutoring a
slow learner.

NOTE: The following re-typed   verbatim from the original
carbon copy.

Saint Joseph Hospital
Ile a la Crosse, Sask.
July 14,1948.

Dr. A. B. Symes,
Regional Supeintendant
Dept. of National Health & Welfare,
Fort Qu'Appelle, Sask.

Dear Dr. Symes:
  Referring you to your letter of July 3rd ult. regarding a chartered trip to Primrose Lake, I beg to submit that you have made a confusion in the names. Primrose Lake is south west of Ile a la Crosse and on the Alberta boundary line and quite far away south west of Pachuanak. I will suggest that you take a look at the air map section Ile a la Crosse. On top of the map you will find Patuanak on the Shaguana Lake, then east on the Churchill River you will find first Dipper Lake then east again <u>Primeau Lake.</u> Stop there. You have arrived at destination.

Patuanak is on the scheduled flight route of Gov. Airways. Hence passenger fare only charged. On the east of Patuanak, flights are charged on charter rate. I was a passenger on that trip of April 14, being called to visit some sick Indians at Patuanak and Primeau Lake. Hence the charge single rate Ile a la Crosse to Patuanak and back to Ile a la Crosse, and chartered rate Patuanak to Primeau Lake and back to Patuanak. Even if I did not have to stop at Patuanak, I would have taken the same way to go to Primeau because it comes cheaper. It gives me the advantage to visit two Indian settlements and the charter trip return would be only 40 miles, while the charter trip Ile a la Crosse to Primeau return is 90 miles permitting to   visit only one Indian settlement.

Yours truly,

P.E. Lavoie, M.D.

It happened   fairly regularly
that Doc's aeroplane would be weathered in
for several days at some tiny hamlet where
he and the pilot would have to hunker down
on the earth floor of a welcoming log
cabin.

Occasionally, over Maman's objections, I
was allowed to go along on a medical trip if
there was space on the aircraft. On one such
trip, we were flying back with a sick woman
from Cree Lake. As we flew over a smallish
lake the pilot yelled over the roar of the
"WACO" biplane's engine.

"Hey, Doc! What the hell is that lying
all over the ice down there?"

Doc looked hard as the pilot flew lower
over the lake.

"It looks like maybe a bunch of caribou
just lying there. But why they are not
moving? Maybe we can land to see what is the
matter?"

Soon the WACO was bumping over the small
crusted drifts that covered the ice. It
stopped near one of the grey-black humps
that littered the lake and we all got out
except the Dene woman patient.

Doc felt the carcass of the caribou. It
had not yet stiffened completely so that he
was able to open the dead animal's mouth
that had stained the snow red with blood.

"My Lord! All they took was the tongue!"

he yelled in   surprise. The two men examined more carcasses. All of them had been recently shot, and their tongues cut out.

"Maudi! Maudi!" Doc kept repeating, damn, angrier than I had ever seen him. "Who could have commit such a criminal waste? Certainly it could not be the Indians."

The pilot who had wandered off some distance away suddenly yelled,

"Come and see this, Doc."

When we got to him over the small drifts, he pointed out the twin tracks that only an aircraft on skis could have made.

"Here's your answer Doc. Somebody landed here beside the herd and whoever was aboard just picked them off one by one with high powered rifles. You can see dozens of empty shell casings just up there a ways. My God! There must be close to a hundred caribou going to waste here."

"Surely the native people could use the meat. We will see what can be done," Doc answered. "Stop at Buffalo on the way, George, because Bill Tunstead, the game warden, is visiting there this week.

Picture of running caribou with aeroplane wing shadow clearly visible in the foreground.

Maybe Bill can radio to Patuanak and Cree Lake to tell the people to go and get the meat."

We did land at Buffalo Narrows and passed the story on to the game warden. He in turn was able to get a radio message to the Hudson Bay Post in Patuanak which was passed on to Père Moreaud. It didn't take him long to get the local people to harness their dogs and head north over the frozen Mudjadik river. But a "cariole" toboggan can only carry about five hundred pounds of meat, so only some of the dead caribou hindquarters were chopped off the frozen carcases and retrieved for the long return trip. The rest of the meat had to be left there to eventually rot. Hopefully, the wolves and foxes managed to eat some of it before the ice broke up.

Is it any wonder that the woodland caribou were disappearing in the North just as the prairie bison had on the southern plains years before?

Mention of Game Warden Tunstead's intervention brings to mind a novel winter conveyance that he introduced into our area with only mixed success. The dog team was a dependable but slow and cold means of travel. The aircraft was fast and, once they enclosed the cockpit, the pilot and passengers were fairly warm. But flying was expensive and still quite primitive, subject to the whims of weather. What's more, the difference between "landing" and "falling" was fairly slight, and that made a number of passengers nervous.

My friend, Mary (Tunstead) Miller, lent me this picture of the "Snow-Planer". The identity of the two men is unknown but the young boy was probably Mary's brother Billy Tunstead.

But an aircraft on skis could taxi along on the ice at a hell of a speed before take-off. Why not build a wingless plane that just stayed on the frozen surface? Thus was born Bill Tunstead's "snowplaner".

When Bill unveiled his highbred combination of aircraft and sled it created quite a stir in the North, plus a certain amount of derisive laughter. The cabin of the craft was somewhat like that of an aeroplane but without a nose or tail section. One big difference from the usual was that the engine and propeller faced backward. A big sheet of steel that swivelled just behind the prop served as a rudder. Bill explained that a "pusher prop" was less likely to blur his vision as he skimmed along on the snow covered ice. The machine could seat two and provided some stowage space. It looked odd, but sleek at the same time.

During the run-up trials that Bill conducted on the ice near shore, we kids had a glorious time leaning against the prop-wash, closing our eyes to the stinging snow. The snowplaner performed reasonably well although it did occasionally make short flights when it hit a high drift too fast. The hubbub even drew Doc to lakeside to watch.

"Hey Doc! This is what you need to visit your patients."

Bill was effusive in   his excitement about
the new toy.

"Come on Doc. There's room for two. I
want to make a run around Grosse Ile and
time it. That's almost five miles according
to the map. I want to see what the
snowplaner can do with a load on."

Doc didn't rise to the sly taunt about
his weight.

"It is not dangerous?" he asked somewhat
tremulously.

"Nah!" Bill reassured him. "You've taxied
in a lot of aeroplanes haven't you? This is
kind of the same thing. Come on! You'll see.
It's alright."

Finally Doc climbed into the second seat
and Bill pulled the loading door closed on
the two of them. I watched in envy as the
engine revved up and the apparatus began to
move onto the lake. Gradually it increased
speed sending up a long cloud of blown snow
behind the prop.

Shortly, the machine disappeared around
the eastern end of Big Island and we began
to watch the western point where we expected
it to reappear before too long.

We watched and we watched but the
snowplaner failed to reappear.

I had decided to go back home to the
mission when someone yelled,

"Look! There they are, walking!"

Finally, I too could make out the two small figures plodding over the crusted snow towards the village.

This was the first of many long walks that Bill Tunstead had from whatever place his cantankerous snow vehicle dumped him. This time, it was a frozen gas line, he said. But every time, it was something else. Once he even tore a ski off the thing when he hit an unseen ice heave about two feet high. He was lucky to get out of that one alive. By break-up, he was ready to sell it or burn it. I was told later that a commercial fisherman finally bought it and hitched it up to his team of ponies. At least the cabin kept him out of the cold wind as he went to pull his nets.

As for Doc, his first snowplaner ride was also his last.

CHAPTER 15:-BREAKUP!

In late March and early April, the lake ice lost its insulating snow cover and the returning sun began to play havoc with the ice surface itself. The ice along the shore of the lake was the first to go and though the ice pan remained solid for a time, it would start to "candle" by mid-April. One could still dog sled on it for a while provided you protected the dogs' feet with leather booties.

Eventually the ice became so rotten that you went on it at your peril. Then is when the ingenuity of the Northerner, who just had to get somewhere, came to the fore. The vehicle of choice was a small clapboard skiff that had its bottom fitted with a couple of sleigh runners. Thus equipped, two or three people could row out from shore to a sturdier looking part of the ice pan. Then with poles and paddles, they would break the edge ice ahead of the little boat until they reached ice solid enough to stand on. At that point they would disembark to pull and push their skiff along the candled ice. They would try to stay away from "black" ice as this indicated it was weak. But, sometimes, no matter how carefully they chose their route, they would break through forcing them to jump back into the boat. Then the process of breaking the weak ice ahead of the boat would resume until they reached another section of stronger ice. Breaking through happened more and more often as the ice aged and many a traveller got back to shore soaked to the waist.

One of Doc's favourite stories was about two Swedes crossing the lake in this way. Martin Bruestead was in the front of the skiff, pulling with the tie up rope while Olie Olafson was at the stern pushing on the transom. Suddenly, Martin felt the ice giving way beneath him and he gave the rope a jerk so he could jump into the safety of the boat. Unfortunately, his quick action had yanked the boat away from his companion leaving poor Olie straddling a widening crack in the ice pan, out of reach of the skiff. Seeing his predicament, Martin yelled,

"Yump Olie! Yump!"

But Olie, desperately trying to keep his balance as his legs spread farther and farther apart, each boot on its particular ice pan, responded quite sensibly,

"Yesus Martin! How can I yump ven I got no place to stood?"

Fortunately, Martin managed to fish his friend out of the freezing water and get him to shore and to a warm fire before he stiffened up completely.

Every time Doc told the story, he would act out Olie's predicament, spreading his legs wider and wider on the floor and waving his arms as an effort to keep his balance.

Then in a paroxysm of laughter, Doc would fall back into his easy chair. The odd intermingling of Swedish and French accents made the story even more hilarious to the listeners.

Towards the end of May, when we boys took our first swim, the water was open enough to permit a boat or canoe to navigate between the ice floes. Occasionally, a person might get "iced in" by converging ice pans, but this usually didn't trap anyone for long as the next breeze or some current action would soon open the channel up again.

One morning, usually in early June, all of the wayward ice would have gone completely. It was then officially Summer.

CHAPTER 16:- CRUISING DOWN THE RIVER

Ah, summertime! How we waited longingly through the winter for it to come back. Then dog teams would be chained up in the bush or turned loose on a convenient small island. One fish net, lifted once a day, was enough to keep the dogs and the family fed.

The village kids, when we weren't actively swimming, would often spend an hour or so line fishing off the "big dock" where the government ferry landed. No fancy pole or other equipment was needed; just a heavy green line and a spooned hook available at the HBC for thirty cents. Tie the end of the line to wrist or ankle and twirl the spooned end around your head several times, and you could cast it out the full fifty feet of the line. Then you would pull it in hand over hand. It was rare that you couldn't catch a fish within three casts. As soon as a boy had enough to feed the family, he would haul his catch home for mother to clean and cook.

If your hook got snagged, you would untie one of the canoes or skiffs, that were tied up to the dock, and pole out to retrieve it, thus saving yourself the cost of a replacement.

Everybody had some kind of boat to travel the waterways with, whether it was a canvas covered canoe or a wooden dory.

By this time, only a few continued to use the paddle or a pair of oars for power. The outboard motor became more and more common. The favourite at first was the "ELTO" 8 horse, probably because it was the least expensive. This particular model had a bevelled pipe behind the drive shaft that was meant to channel the exhaust and some of the noise down into the water. The first thing one did on acquiring an ELTO was to cut a big hole into this so-called muffler pipe because in doing so, one gained a considerable increase in speed as the action of pushing all that exhaust into the water wasted power, or so it seemed. The result is that you could hear a motor coming a mile away, and all you had to do was find the long plume of oily smoke behind the boat to locate its position.

Even the still popular canoe was adapted to the outboard motor by having a "V" shaped transom inserted into the pointed back end. This tended to lift the front dangerously high if you didn't have a counterweight in the bow. A biggish rock might do, but not too big because, again, you would get more speed if the canoe "planed" just right with only the rear half of the canoe skimming the water. This desire for speed sometimes led to a spill if an errant wind happened to whip the bow around. The life jacket was either unknown or ignored back then. We nearly lost a few young men as a result of this kind of "hot-dogging".

We came close to losing others whenever a boater's "kicker" became a stubborn lump of inert metal, refusing to start. One day, for example, my friends and I watched old Louis Bijeault, the fur trader from Canoe Lake, try to start his outboard motor near the government dock. We were swimming at the time, but soon our attention was drawn to old Louis' efforts to start his machine. Time after time, he would wrap the starting rope around the flywheel and give it a vicious yank, to no avail. Every few pulls, he would make an adjustment to his needle valve or the spark lever and try again. What caught our attention particularly was the flow of French cuss words that accompanied every unsuccessful attempt.

"Maudit enfant de chienne!" he'd yell at the motor. "Qu'est çe que tu as donc?" (Damn S.O.B! What's wrong with you.)

But the motor passively got even for being called "son of a bitch" and other names by continued inactivity.

Several times the spark plugs were screwed out and cleaned. Then the carburettor was disassembled and blown in and re-installed in the process of which Louis suffered a nasty cut from a screwdriver that slipped. But nothing worked.

Finally, when pull after pull failed to bring the motor to life, we watched Louis loosen the clamps that held the motor to the transom. Then we saw the old man lift the

Elto high above his head and throw it into the lake with a shout of,

"Que le Diable t'emporte!" (Devil take you!)

I watched to see if there was some sign that the devil had accepted the proffered gift but there was none unless it was the rainbow colours caused by the thin film of gasoline that floated to the surface. Then Louis paddled his boat back to the dock, tied up, and strode away to the village muttering damnation to all mechanical devices as he went.

As for us kids, we resumed playing water tag, repeating "enfant de chienne" and several other choice invectives we had just learned. We were still playing in the water over an hour later when we saw old Louis plodding back to the wharf.

Looking a bit embarrassed, he asked,

"You boys, you tink you can maybe dive to find dat moteur dat fell in de lake, eh? I'm give two dollar to de one he can find h'it and bring h'it to me."

This produced a mad hurricane of splashing bodies for a few minutes. One-eyed Jimmy was the lucky one to find the motor and with the help of a couple of others, managed to lift it up to Louis waiting in his skiff. After paying off the diver, Louis hefted the kicker onto his shoulder and headed off towards   Vic Marquis' shop.

When I told Doc about the incident, he said it was lucky old Bijeault had not suffered a heart attack, because his "other kicker" was in bad shape too.

The medical canoe with, L-R, Emile, Doc's brother Omer, Maman and Bebe, Doc with his pipe and Rene at the tiller.

Doc himself had been provided with a 22 foot freighter canoe by the health authorities. It had an extra wide body for carrying patients, when necessary, and was thus fairly stable. Unfortunately it was under-powered with just a 9 horse Johnson kicker. With any kind of a load, it was a long trip to anywhere.

Doc, however, having been raised by the Gulf of Saint Lawrence, wanted "un vrai bateau", a real boat, complete with a deck and a cabin, disdaining the smaller craft as too small and tippy to be comfortable. He kept looking at boat brochures and dreaming of somehow importing a cabin cruiser from down East. But the cost and the problem of getting the vessel delivered stymied his dream.

Up in Buffalo Narrows, however, lived Tom Pederson who had learned boat building in his native Norway. He had built himself a small inboard cabin boat that he used to tow a little scow hauling freight or iced fish around the Buffalo lakes. Time came, however, when Tom's business outgrew his capacity. He needed bigger all around.

On a routine visit to Buffalo Narrows, Doc learned that Tom was building himself a new boat with Frank Nordstrom's help and might be looking to sell his other one. Before long, Tom was showing Doc through the vessel, explaining its operation and defending its seaworthiness. There was a fair sized cabin with two bunks forward and a bit of a galley aft. The inboard motor was covered with a big wooden box that doubled as the galley table.

Finally, when it seemed like it might be time to get down to serious negotiations, Tom unlocked his storage locker in the bow and brought out a forty ounce of scotch. I wasn't there but Tom's son, Skipper, popped in to see if the two of them were coming for supper. They were both by then "two sheets in the wind", to use a nautical expression, and not in the least   interested in food.

Skipper told me later on that it was the most mixed up conversation he had ever heard. What with Doc's French accent and Tom's Norwegian accent, they were both having problems understanding one another and each tried to clarify things in either French or Norwegian,

Mais, Tom, is it not trop petit for the big lakes? I would be scare it might, how you say, "renversé" in a big wind, no?

"Vel, Doc! Yust a minute. This vessel can take any kind of vind! Don' you vorry 'bout dat. By yimminy, I could cross the North Sea to Norvay in vinter vithout problem! I build dis boat to float, not to zink!

Skipper left them still bargaining. A bit later, when he looked out towards the wharf, the boat was gone. Evidently, the time for a demonstration ride had come.

The two sailors were gone overnight and well into the next day. It was near noon when they came ashore both suffering from the "forty ounce flu" as Skipper called it. Neither was too sure of the immediate past.

Apparently, they had both woken up on the boat that morning, drifting gently, not knowing where they were nor which course to take to get back to civilisation. They were in the middle of a very big body of water where neither shore was clearly visible.

So Tom cranked up the ageing inboard and headed generally south by compass thinking that they were either on Big Buffalo or Lac Clair given the size of the swells. Doc contented himself by sitting on the poop deck thankful for the fresh air and occasional dash of spray that cooled his fevered head. Finally Tom recognised a few landmarks and steered at last through Keizie Channel and into the Buffalo Narrows boat dock area.

They were both still a little unsteady on their sea legs as they walked up to Tom's house. A couple of pots of strong coffee later, they felt almost human and concluded the deal on the sale of the boat. Doc christened it the "Mal de Mer" and couldn't wait to get it to Ile a la Crosse.

"Skipper, you maybe better go along vith Doc to show him how she handles," Tom decided." Check the gas and the oil to make sure she'll make it."

They cast off in mid-afternoon towing Doc's freighter canoe behind them. Once they were in the calm of Deep River, Doc was feeling better and better and took over the helm from Skipper. He couldn't resist stopping off at Ausland's Deep River Fur Farm to show off his acquisition. Doc had his first mishap when he grounded before he could reach the small dock on which Halvor Ausland, another Norwegian, stood with a puzzled look on his face.

"Doc? Is that you? Vot in hell are you doing in Tom Pederson's boat for crissakes? Throw me a rope and I'll pull you in closer if you and Skipper step to the back."

This done, nothing would do but to go up to the Ausland house for coffee and smoked herring. Doc accepted the brew but his recovering stomach couldn't face the fish, a specialty that Halvor had just got from Norway.

Now vy in hell vould you buy that tub from Tom Pederson? Yust you vait, Doc, you'll regret it. That boat vas built for towing and she'll be hard to handle in a vind vithout a load to pull." He totally ignored Skipper who stood there listening with a smile on his face to all the scorn being heaped on the boat his Dad had built.

Doc had seldom met two Scandinavians who could stand one another's guts and the Ausland/Pederson relationship was no exception. So Doc took Halvor's dire predictions with a grain of salt.

Soon it was time to sail on. With the engine revved up in full reverse, and both Doc and Skipper poling with all their strength, they were able to get the boat off the river bottom to continue down river towards Lac Ile-a-la-Crosse.

A few minutes later, they met P'ti Louis Morin heading North in his big skiff and they stopped to chat. Doc was feeling so

confident in his   boat handling
ability by this time that he insisted that
Skipper go back home to Buffalo with P'ti
Louis. Skipper was a bit hesitant but
finally allowed himself to be talked into
making the return trip with P'ti Louis.

As it turned out, this was a mistake!

Soon after Doc got under way again and
P'ti Louis' skiff was out of sight, Doc's
nostrils picked up the scent of scorching
paint. Turning from the wheel, he could see
heat waves rising from the engine cover.
Quickly he stopped engine and lifted the
cover to a cloud of smoke coming from the
overheated machine.

Doc had a reputation as a very competent
surgeon, but he was no mechanic. What's more
all he could find on board was an old pair
of pliers. With this, he did manage to get
one of the water hoses off without scalding
himself too badly. Obviously, the system had
run dry. Doc tried to pour a bit of water
into the hose and the water jacket. After he
reassembled the hose, he re-started the
engine, but not for long as it immediately
started to heat up again.

Finally, he had to admit defeat. He
pulled up the canoe that he had been towing
and reversed the position and function of
the two vessels.

Thus it was that on his very first trip
on Mal de Mer, he ended up ignominiously

towing it into Ile a   la Crosse behind the canoe.

Vic Marquis was called in to find the trouble, which he soon did. A water intake pipe below the surface that was supposed to bring in cooling water to the engine had become plugged up somehow. It was then that Doc remembered the grounding the boat had suffered at Ausland's landing. No doubt in the effort of pushing it off, the boat had dug into the river bottom and fouled the cooling system intake.

Mal de Mer on one of it's ill fated trips.

Every time he took the boat out he ran into a problem. He got hung up on both the Canoe River and the Beaver River because his draught was too much for these relatively shallow streams.

Just as Halvor Ausland had predicted, the little cabin cruiser was battered about by any wind above a strong breeze to the point where Doc often lost the ability to steer

her in any direction   except downwind. He
ended up several times headed unwillingly
down the length of South Bay pushed by a
strong north wind that would not allow him
to get back to Ile a la Crosse.

After her first few trips, each of which
ended up in some sort of calamity, Maman
absolutely refused to set foot on board ever
again. Even Doc began to show stress, to the
point where he sometimes talked to Mal de
Mer in French, English and even Latin- and
he wasn't praying.

Little by little, Mal de Mer was left to
wallow idly at dockside as Doc returned to
using the big medical canoe. If the nine
horse kicker ever did quit on him, he could
at least revert to using the paddle until he
met help somewhere on the waterway.

Eventually, Doc was provided with a speedboat equipped
with a 22hp Johnson motor. Its white colour made it
visible from miles away and it was immediately christened
the Pelican. It shortened boat trips considerably.

CHAPTER 17:-ON STORMY SEAS

Doc wasn't the only one to experience problems afloat. One particular summer, our cousins George Paquette and Martin Senechal had been invited to spend the summer holidays with us. They were both René's age, about 15, and though the three of them tolerated having 12 year old Emile tag along on their adventures, they all made it obvious that they drew the line at a pain in the ass little 9 year old brother spoiling their fun. But no matter how often they told me to get lost, it was pretty hard for them, in a small village, to get very far away from me. Thus I was a witness to the day of the raft.

Walking along the beach that day, they found part of a boat dock washed up on shore. This wasn't unusual as every spring the moving ice always managed to dislodge several docks. What was unusual in this instance was the size of the thing. Pushing it out into the lake, they found that their instant raft could float two of them comfortably, but it would start to sink if a third person tried to get on.

Martin suggested they make a bigger raft out of it by adding whatever they could to increase its cargo capacity. So it became a project with all of us, even me, searching for scraps of wood that could be added to the craft.

"Bébé, go to the shed and get a hammer

and some big nails," René ordered.

I was off like a flash, my heart pounding with delight at being included in any way in the construction. Opening the shed door I stuffed my pockets so full of rusty spikes that my pants threatened to descend to my knees. Grabbing a hammer, I started out with my load but Doc stopped me in my tracks.

"Ou va-tu avec tout ça?" he asked noting the hammer and bulging pockets.

I wasn't sure that he would approve of what was planned so I tried to be as vague as I could.

"Les gars veulent arranger quelque chose" I stammered thinking that "wanting to fix something" was indefinite enough and truthful enough to be acceptable.

Doc hesitated but decided to let the matter drop with a caution to me not to lose his hammer again.

I raced back to the shore, excitement making me oblivious to the pain of several nails sticking me in the thighs as I ran.

The four boys had made some progress while I was gone. They had lashed two fair sized logs to either side of the main platform. With the help of my burden of nails, an extra decking of boards was fastened across the width. In no time we were ready for launching.

First we had to look around for some poles to be used for propulsion. I found a beauty that had washed up against the government wharf and proudly carried it back to the raft. But my elation was cut short when Marty commandeered my long pole and began prying the raft off the shore into deeper water with it. Emile had found an old paddle with half the blade missing. With George and René up to their knees in the water pulling on a short piece of rope tied to one end of the raft and with me pushing with all my might at the back, at last the raft floated free, and the four older boys jumped on.

But when I tried to embark, René stopped me.

"There's no room for you, Bébé," he said. Then at sight of my crestfallen face and brimming eyes he quickly added,

"But you'll get a turn later. O.K.?"

Well it was anything but O.K. with me and for an hour I sat on the big dock silently but fervently praying that they would all fall off and drown as they poled and paddled "our" raft around without me.

They were careful at first to stay near shore but as they became more confident in their ability to control the craft they got out deeper and deeper with Marty poling at the stern and Emile using his half paddle as a steering mechanism in the front. They were so engrossed in their sailing adventure that they didn't notice the black clouds forming in the west.

They were just about at the maximum permissible depth for their pole to reach when the wind hit.

Delightedly, I watched the chaos developing on board as the four sailors realised their predicament.

"Marty, for Pete's sake push us back towards shore!" René yelled.

But Marty was already on his belly trying at arm's length to reach bottom with the pole, which had suddenly become much too short.

"I can't reach! The pole isn't long enough!" he cried.

Then George piped up with, "Maybe you can use it like an oar while Emile paddles."

There was a lot of splashing but it had little effect against the wind. The waves had become high enough to start washing over the deck by this time and Marty slipped and fell losing the pole in the process.

I watched in delight as they drifted farther and farther out, thanking whichever divinity had produced the storm in answer to my prayer.

Between the peals of thunder and flashes

of lightning I could   just make out René's
faint yell.

"Bébé, go and get somebody with a boat to
help us."

"But don't get Doc," Emile was quick to
add.

George was kneeling on the deck of the
raft rocking back and forth, obviously near
tears while Marty had taken over the half-
paddle from Emile. With this he was
desperately digging through the waves, not
conscious of the fact that he was only
managing to make the raft turn in the water
like a heaving merry-go-round.

"What did you say?" I yelled, "I can't
hear you!"

Frankly, I enjoyed the lie and the
feeling of power it gave me.

As the rain began to pelt down, I decided
to run home for shelter.

"Don't tell Doc, huh. No room for me huh.
I'll show them" I whispered to myself in a
fine dander!

Maman met me at the door and immediately
made me take off my wet shirt.

"Ou sont René et les autres?" she asked
worriedly. "Ils vont être tout trempe dans
cette orage!" (Where are René and the others?

They'll get totally soaked in this
downpour.)

Frankly I thought that getting wet from
the rain was the least of the boys'
problems.

"Ils sont dans le lac," I admitted " sur
notre 'raft'", not knowing the French word
for it.

"Quoi? Dans le lac par une tempète
pareille?"(What? On the Lake in such a
storm?)

She ran to the living room crying,
"Docteur, vien vite. Les garçons sont au
large dans le lac!" (Doctor, come quickly!
The boys are out on the lake.)

Doc had been snoozing in his chair and
was rubbing the sleep from his eyes.

"Maudi, ques-ce-qui ce passe? Dit moi
vite!"(Damn, what's going on? Tell me
quick!)

All restraints gone, I burst into tears
and stammered out the whole story.

I had never seen Doc move so fast.
Donning his rubber boots he hurried out.
Quickly putting on the dry shirt Maman
insisted I wear, I was out the door after
him. Oblivious to the storm, Doc was at
dockside in no time and he could just make
out the raft and its occupants out in the
middle of the lake.

Fortunately, Auguste Durocher had seen Doc rush past his house and, sensing that there was something wrong, followed closely behind ignoring the pelting rain. In no time he had launched Doc's big canoe and he and Doc splashed through the waves towards the quartet.

With the violence of the storm abating to some degree, they managed to get the four boys into the canoe. Fearing that such a big piece of flotsam might constitute a danger to boat traffic, Doc had Auguste lash a rope to the raft and they towed it back to shore.

As they disembarked from the canoe Doc said, menacingly, "René, va chercher la hache."

Taking off at a dead run, René was back in no time with the axe. The storm was over, but soon the noise of splintering wood replaced the thunder.

Between Doc and Auguste, the raft was reduced to small pieces as the chips flew from repeated blows. All five of us looked on glumly during the destruction, afraid to say a word.

Then, axe in hand, Doc went back to the house without a backward glance. Timidly, the five of us followed.

I tried hard to hide my smile!

CHAPTER 18:-TREATY AND OTHER PARTIES.

Waiting for Treaty Payment.

Despite all the problems he'd had with the little cabin cruiser, Doc's friendship with Tom Pederson, the used boat salesman, strengthened and the two could often be heard singing off-key in two languages aboard Tom's newer and bigger tug-boat.

Tom had also built a big covered scow for his freighting business and this rig was contracted every summer by Indian Affairs to transport treaty payment officials to the various Indian Reserves accessible by water.

Tom Pederson's covered barge. It made a comfortable accommodation for Treaty Party. members.

The covered scow could sleep and feed up to ten people in reasonable comfort at various landing places such as Patuanak, Turner Lake, La Loche and Dillon. As Doc was always included on these expeditions, I yearned to go with him as I had heard that "Treaty Days" was a fun experience. The answer from Maman was always, "non, non, non!"

Tom's son, Skipper, usually went along as chief engineer and helmsman on the tug on these so-called "Treaty Parties" leaving Tom free to socialise aboard the "house-boat" scow.

Fortunately, Skipper always knew where they were.

Finally, when I was 14, Doc agreed that I could go along on the Patuanak leg, particularly when Skipper said I could bunk in with him in the tug itself.

Doc and a couple of nurses always went along with the Treaty Party to do a comprehensive health survey at each landing. Tuberculosis was still endemic in those days and early detection was thought to be the key to a cure. But the Indians feared the cure more than they did the disease, as this might involve a long stay away from their people at a southern sanatorium. Often, Doc had to have the Mounted Police escort accompany him to a cabin where he suspected an infected person might be hiding. But he got most of them with his stethoscope as they lined up to receive their treaty money. The two nurses would collect saliva swabs and small samples of blood for later analysis.

Noblesse oblige! Doc gave up his boots and hip waders so that the Treaty Party nurses could keep their feet dry on a wet landing.

The R.C.M.P. Constable, in full scarlet regalia, was always responsible for the satchel full of crisp new dollar bills which he would hand over, five at a time, to the head Indian Agent seated with him at the folding table.

Treaty Party team in a relaxed moment. Note the RCMP'S footwear. Doc felt the occasion demanded full dress; jacket, vest, tie and Fedora hat!

Each recipient had to identify himself by both his Indian and his Christian name as well as his Indian Affairs number. An interpreter was always along to ask questions and glean information about family and status.

Sometimes, a man might not even be sure if he was "treaty" or not. It all depended on whether his great grand-father had made his X on the treaty parchment or had accepted the land scrip instead. If the latter was the case, that automatically, magically, somehow made him and all his

descendants "white men". This led to a
lot of consultation in voices that always
got louder and louder in the effort of
making the white man understand Dene or Cree
as if sheer volume might get through his
cranium if logic could not. Unfortunately,
the Indian Agent and his official lists had
the last word and even the chief could not
change the outcome, no matter how eloquent
he sounded.

The Dene people did not traditionally
have chiefs in the ordinary sense. Each
extended family was a unit unto itself
always led by consensus of all the men in
the group. But the white fur traders wanted
to deal with whoever was considered the
leading man, usually the oldest, and then
would ensure that man's future loyalty by
giving him a suit of clothes and gifts of
gunpowder and tobacco and calling him "le
Capitaine".

In no time, this idea of a chief became a
part of Chipewyan culture and was ritually
carried on by the Indian Agents who would
clothe the recognised chief of each group
with a new suit of clothes each year. He
also got an extra ten crisp dollar bills
added to the usual five, this to replace the
gifts of tobacco and gunpowder.

A semi-dressed Chief with the 'real' boss. He must have lost his yellow striped trousers.

The honour of being chief was generously passed on fairly regularly from one old person to another so that he too might get all decked out in a black suit complete with yellow stripes down each pant leg. These stripes were meant to symbolise policeman type power but no one in the tribe really recognised the chief's authority.

After the men were paid their treaty dollars, it was the turn of the women to line up for payment each with her children. This was a slower procedure as Doc insisted on giving each one a thorough examination. The introduction of sweets into the diet of Northern people had led to a lot of decayed teeth. All Doc could do was yank these out as drilling and filling were beyond his capability. Again a stern look from the booted and spurred Mounty was often needed to convince a child to open his or her mouth. The nurses passed out free toothbrushes with instructions on the use being demonstrated and then elaborated by the interpreter.

Another Indian Reserve, another Treaty Party.
Bill Tunstead is standing behind Doc. The
names of the rest of the group, including the
dog, are not known.

Each birth that had occurred since the
previous year was duly recorded and Indian
Affairs numbers assigned to the newborns.
Doc was particularly interested in the
condition of the new mothers as giving birth
weakened them to the point that they were
more susceptible to infection with
tuberculosis. Each nursing mother received a
small package containing powdered milk and
other food supplements in an effort to
decrease the rate of infant mortality. Doc
was embarrassed by its pitiful inadequacy,
but he was helpless to squeeze more from a
government struggling with the cost of the
war.

When payment and medical processing was completed, the whole group was invited to the traditional feast. Doc and the rest learned to relish boiled red sucker heads, baked beaver tail and even, on occasion, a portion of a caribou head that had been roasted over a hot fire with the hide and hair still on.

Skipper and I stuck to filling up with some "les beignes", not really doughnuts but a type of bannock, often with blueberries added to the dough, and cut into strips to be deep fried in lard or bear grease. Dipped into corn syrup or sugar, the resultant hot delicacy easily filled every internal cavity.

After the feast, the guitars and violins were unwrapped and the dancing would begin. This was the cue for the missionary priest to get lost and for the caches of "tchepwegees" to be tapped. This home brew's ingredients depended on which berries mother nature had provided in quantity that year and what the brewer might find in his larder to spice up the hooch. It was never very potent, but Doc said that if you could force a large enough volume down without throwing up, you might experience a bit of a high.

When the "party was getting a glow on, and singing filled the air", it was time for all the whities to head back to the house-boat and some real booze.

Somewhat reluctantly, Skipper and I headed for our bunks in the tug. I was asleep before long, dreaming that a huge rock had been placed on my stomach. Too many fried bannocks!

Some time later, I felt a hand shaking my shoulder and I heard Skipper whisper,

"Bébé, wake up! You've got to come and hear this."

Still half asleep I followed him to the fantail of the house-boat.

Signalling me to be silent, Skipper opened the cabin door a bit and cupped his ear in a listening signal.

I put my ear near the crack in the door to be nearly deafened by the cacophony of snores coming from the interior.

It sounded a bit like an orchestra that badly needed tuning and a conductor. I immediately recognised Doc's heavy tuba backed up by increasingly higher pitched brass horns from the other men. And behind their privacy wall of a hanging blanket, the soprano treble of the two nurses tuned in in two-four time.

It was all Skipper and I could do to keep ourselves from laughing out loud. Unfortunately, recording equipment was not yet in common use at that time and the Moonlight "Snorata" was lost to posterity.

CHAPTER 19:-"IF THE OCEAN WAS WHISKEY!"

And I was a duck, I'd swim to the bottom, And never come up. (From an old drinking song)

"What is the next case, Pete?"

"Bootlegging, Doc. Caught the guy selling whiskey to a native. Emile Benoit was a witness."

Pete Nightingale was the RCMP corporal in charge of the Ile a la Crosse police detachment consisting of himself, one regular RCMP Constable, and one Special Constable. These three men were responsible for maintaining law and order in that part of the North in the mid 40's.

Peculiarly, even though prohibition had ended in most areas of Saskatchewan by that time, in the North it lived on in spirit (no pun intended). Liquor offences, and the consequences thereof, constituted most of the cases to appear before Justice of the Peace, Doc Lavoie. Doc was also the official coroner and so was often involved in legal proceedings in the North.

"Eh bien" call in the accused one and the witness." ordered the JP.

Corporal Nightingale summoned the two men into his office and read off the charge.

"Isidore Saint- Brieux, you are
charged with illegally selling liquor to
Magloire Courtemanche on the evening of
February 11ᵗʰ, 1942 in the pool room operated
by Emile Benoit. How do you plead? Guilty or
not guilty." Evidently, buying illegal
liquor was legal, but selling it was not!

"Hey, Doc, you know me. I didn't do
nothing wrong. Honest to God, Doc!" Isidore,
more commonly known as "Izzy" made his plea
directly to the JP.

"Yes, I surely know you well by now,
Izzy. So you are saying you are not guilty
of selling booze to Magloire? And remember,
you are suppose to call me Your Honneur
during the trial."

"For sure I'm not guilty, Doc, 'scuse me,
I mean Your Honour."

"Caporale Nightingale, what is the
evidence in this case?"

"Well, Your Honour, we have the witness,
Emile Benoit, who will testify to what he
saw. Mister Benoit, please stand and put
your hand on the book. Do you swear to tell
the truth so help you God?"

"I do!"

"Allo, Emile! Ça va?" Doc greeted his old
friend who, with his wife, Julia, ran the
only hotel, restaurant, and pool room in the
village. He was also the Postmaster.

162

"Pas mal, merci, Doc", the hotelier responded.

Nightingale began the questioning.

"Will you tell the Justice of the Peace what you saw happening in your pool room the afternoon of February 11th last?"

"Well I was just going into the pool room when I saw Izzy slip what looked like a bottle to Magloire who put it into his parka pocket. And I saw Magloire give Izzy some money."

"Do we have that bottle, Caporal?

"Yes, Your Honour." Nightingale responded. I was sitting in the café in the booth near the door when Magloire was going out. As he passed, I heard something in his pocket clunk when it hit the booth and it gurgled like it was a bottle. So I stopped Magloire and confiscated this bottle which I now enter as evidence. Magloire insisted it wasn't his. He was just carrying it for Izzy, he said. I can call Magloire in to testify if you like Your Honour."

His Honour was carefully studying the evidence.

"I see this bottle was open before because the seal is broken and it look like there is some gone. Are you certain that this is liquor Caporal?"

"Well it's in a liquor bottle, and the

contents are the colour of whiskey, Doc, I mean Your Honour."

" Well many things are that colour you know, Pete. For example it could be strong tea or Indian cough medicine maybe."

"Hey, that's what it is, Doc Your Honour!", Izzy quickly put in. "Strong tea like you said. I gave it to Magloire to keep him warm in his toboggan going back to Sandy Pointe. It was real cold that day, remember?"

Doc decided to uncap the bottle and have a whiff.

"Well it smell maybe like whisky but maybe not," he said. "Have you got a glass or cup so we can have a taste?" he asked the bemused policeman who readily provided the JP with a glass.

Doc poured himself a stiff jolt and sipped, then swished, then drained the glass to the bottom.

"Well I am not certain. Emile, you taste it and tell me if you are certain it is alcoholic."

The policeman produced another glass into which the chief witness poured a generous portion from the suspect bottle.

"Well, Doc, I can't swear that it is for sure liquor. It could be, like you said, very strong, sweet tea."

"Well let us taste some more to make sure. Caporal, maybe you should have a taste too."

Magically another glass appeared in the policeman's hand.

In the end, the Justice of the Peace declared Izzy "Not guilty for lack of evidence!"

"Case dismissed!" he added in a somewhat slurred voice.

Doc always said that more citizens took to drinking during prohibition than during any other period before or since. He joked that when prohibition finally ended, many could only imbibe hard liquor with a dab of smelly limburger cheese below their nostrils, so accustomed were they to surreptitious drinking in the lavatory. All that the continued controls on liquor consumption in the North did was to add to its desirability, its mystique.

Some of the steps taken to make sure that northerners were protected from demon drink seem ludicrous, thinking back. For instance, pressure was put on the stores to keep such items as lemon extract and Aqua Velva shaving lotion off their shelves. Nor could you legally ferment any kind of liquid with the purpose of producing alcohol.

The result of this temperance mentality was to prompt people to play games with the

law, inventing all manner of ways to
get a bit high. Anything deemed to contain
alcohol was subject to experimenting,
sometimes with dangerous results. For
example two young men discovered this when
they tried to filter some liquid boot polish
through a thick slice of bread, thinking
thus to eliminate any poisons that might be
denaturing the hoped for alcohol. Both had
to have their stomachs pumped.

But a confirmed boozer was always willing
to take a chance. Take the case of old Dick
Kirby. For years Dick had kept a stopping
place at the mouth of the Beaver River where
it emptied into Lac Ile a la Crosse. Any
wind-bound water traveller could be assured
of a place on the rough floor by the stove
for his sleeping bag and a filling meal of
salt pork and eggs with credible home-made
buns put up by the "best dang camp cook in
the bush" according to Dick.

There were also barn stalls provided for
the winter swing teams as they came by,
where the freighters could unharness and
rest their horses.

The "relief built" wagon road that had
been cut through the bush from Meadow Lake
to Fort Black on the south shore of Ile a la
Crosse lake eventually led to replacing
horses with freight trucks. But old Dick
stayed on, playing willing host to anybody
who chose to stop at his place for a visit
and a meal.

One day, Doc and I landed at Dick's place as we were returning by canoe from Beauval. The old man was as effusive as ever and insisted that we have a bite to eat.

"But first, Doc, let me show you something."

He rummaged around in a cupboard and set a fairly large square bottle on the long oilcloth covered table. The label clearly read "Rawleigh's Horse Liniment"

"I found a whole case of this stuff in the old barn last week and do you know what Doc? It's pure alcohol! Watch and I'll show you," saying which he poured some into a tablespoon and, striking a wooden match, set it to burning with a gentle blue flame.

"What d'ya think, Doc. Pure alcohol, isn't it?"

"Well yes, it must be mostly alcohol," Doc agreed, "but did you drink any of it?"

"Well you're darn rights I did, two or three bottles so far. Makes a helluva good hot toddy with a little sugar." boasted the old man laughing in glee.

"So that is the proof I need that it is not dangerous because you are obviously not dead, nor are you blind from the effects of drinking this horse medicine."Doc observed.

"But you know, Dick, you should be more careful what you drink because wood alcohol that is poison also burns with a blue flame like that."

The old fellow just laughed at this revelation.

"Well, the proof's in the pudding, Doc. So come on. Let me fix you a hot toddy before supper. You must've got cold travelling on the river today."

Several bottles of liniment were polished off before, during, and after our spaghetti and meat ball meal. It was eventually decided that it was too windy and getting too dark to chance crossing the lake that night. I fell asleep sitting at the big table while I was playing solitaire with a worn old deck of cards that Dick produced for me. Doc woke up with a headache, next morning, sitting in a rocking chair by the still warm cook-stove. Old Dick was snoring happily in his feather bed. All was right with his world!

They both had a shot of "the hair of the dog that bit you" before we embarked for home.

As for Maman, she just would not understand the decree against making your own wine. She kept a twenty gallon crock going fairly constantly by the wood stove in

the kitchen. To   her, wine was not
alcohol. Why, even "le bon Jésus" had made
wine at Cana. How could it be against the
law to ferment some chokecherry or
raspberry juice so that she could serve a
nice glass of wine with dinner?

I recall my two brothers and I being put
to work, one time, collecting several
million dandelion flowers which ended up in
Maman's fermenting crock.

That particular batch of dandelion wine
led to a funny episode that Doc relished
recounting to any visitor.

The once yellow flowers had been removed
from the must and when the fermentation had
ceased, it was decided that the wine had
clarified enough to be siphoned off into
bottles. This job Doc always reserved to
himself so that he could check the quality
of the product from time to time.

The siphoning was stopped about three
inches from the bottom in order to avoid
stirring up the yeasty sediment.

Doc ordered René and Emile to carry the
crock behind the shed and dump the residue.
They seemed to be gone for quite a long
time. Finally I was told to go and see what
was holding them up.

I returned in a few minutes to reveal
that Emile was sick and had thrown up all
over himself and that René was walking and

talking funny. Doc hurried off to discover his two older boys sloshed out of their gourds from the dandelion wine dregs.

Dragging them by their shirt collars he brought them straight to the bathroom where they each got a cold bath and a hot tongue lashing from Maman. As for Doc, he just laughed, contenting himself with telling them that he hoped they had learned their lesson.

Sheepishly, they went to bed to sleep it off while I wondered what had made my brothers act so strangely.

Doc himself wasn't averse to experimentation in the production of strong drink. With the help and encouragement of the government agriculture agencies, he had planted and grown several varieties of fruit trees to see if they were hardy enough to grow and produce in the short, sunny, northern summer. One year, his crab-apple trees produced more fruit than all my friends could snitch. It was in every way a bumper crop, but what could be done with all that fruit?

That was when Doc decided to try brewing some hard apple cider. With the help of the mission carpenter, he built a small wine press and my friend Jimmy One-Eye and I spent a couple of days picking the fruit off the over-laden branches. Then turning the screw on top of the press we watched the juices squirt out into Maman's big washtub.

At last, enough juice had been squeezed to fill the 20 gallon crock. Doc floated a yeast cake on a thick slice of bread at the top of the brew and we all waited. Before long the froth indicating active fermentation appeared and Doc could discern a bit of a hit in an occasional spoonful. Possibly he waited too long to rack the must, hoping, perhaps, to ensure maximum kick.

Eventually, Doc woefully had to confirm Maman's verdict that all our effort had produced 20 gallons of crab-apple vinegar.

This disappointing result was followed some time later by the exploding beer adventure.

One day, Emile Benoit received a strange, heavy parcel in the mail addressed to Doc. With the collusion of a relative still living in free-wheeling Quebec, Doc had ordered a gallon can of malt, suitable for making beer.

Carefully, Doc read the directions written in French and proceeded to establish his own mini-brewery. Soon the rich smell of fermenting beer filled the kitchen, much to Maman's disgust. Wine was blessed by God Himself. But beer, she insisted, was the invention of the Devil!

Meanwhile Doc had enlisted me and my

friends to collect and wash all the beer bottles we could find. Even pop bottles would do. Doc had somehow acquired some press-on bottle caps and a gizmo for securing the caps securely to the filled bottles.

Maybe it was Maman's opposition to the smell. Or it could have been Doc's experience of waiting too long to bottle the apple-jack. Anyway, Doc bottled and capped the wildest batch of beer ever brewed.

The finished product was carefully stowed in the stone lined cellar beneath the house where it was cool.

Several nights later, we were awakened by the sound of sporadic explosions coming from below us. In fact, we could even feel shards of glass imbedding themselves on the floor boards beneath our beds.

Some of the bottles did survive to regale Doc's palate, long denied this pleasure. But serving the brew was quite a production, and Doc often entertained his friends with something akin to a Chinese tea ceremony, only with his home-made beer.

As soon as any visitor was seated, I got my orders.

"Bébé, va me chercher deux bouteilles dans la cave, et amène la grande chaudière."

I was always excited at the prospect of the adventure to come and soon produced the requisite two bottles of beer and the large milk pail.

I would watch as Doc carefully placed the two bottles in the pail and, as quickly as he could, snapped off the caps.

Instantly, the pail was magically filled with foam.

"In a few minutes," Doc would explain to his visitor," the foam will die down and we can enjoy a good glass of beer, French-Canadian style."

I managed to sneak a taste, once, which convinced me to stick with Orange Crush for the time being.

The last word on this boozy chapter must be reserved to the event that resulted in my being teased as "home-brew Bill" for many years.

It was a year when we experienced a fantastic raspberry crop. Even after Maman had decided she had enough canned fruit with over a hundred quarts, there were still lots of berries in the bush, hot and sweet from the summer sun. One day, a bunch of us pre-teens had wandered over to McKay's Point, a favourite site for berry picking.

When Jean-Marie, Chummy, Jimmy One-Eye, Charlie and I had gorged ourselves on berries, we found a bucket that had been left behind by a previous picker. Out of sheer boredom we decided to fill it with the fruit we were too full to eat. But, what to do with these surplus berries? I think it was Charlie who suggested that maybe we could make a batch of "tsepwegese", the Cree word for home-made wine.

In no time we were organised. Jimmy would cover the berries with water while Chummy would get some sugar. I ran home and back in no time with a purloined yeast cake and a slice of bread to float it on. Jean- Marie, who often wore two shirts in case one got torn, gave up a shirt to cover the bucket with.

Swearing one another to secrecy, we went home in anticipation of…what? We weren't sure, but we knew it was illegal and that we'd go to jail if the police caught us.

But we couldn't resist going back every day to our secret hiding place to see if anything was happening.

Sure enough, I soon recognised the foamy froth I had often seen in Maman's wine crock. I had a hard time to convince my buddies that it was too soon to do any sampling; that we would have to be patient and stir the bucket every day until the frothing stopped. Chummy, who lived the closest, eagerly volunteered to be the official stirrer.

The enticement must have been too great for poor Chummy and he apparently started to do some tasting each time he did the stirring. On one such occasion, he must have gone a bit overboard with his sampling because, later that day, Special Constable Léon Bélanger saw him acting strangely in front of some girls and boasting to them that he was drunk.

The long arm of the law soon had him by the collar and it wasn't long before Chummy was singing like a loon.

We were all rounded up and stood before a grim faced Corporal Nightingale within sight of the waiting iron bars.

The policeman began with a tirade in a loud voice.

"The Doctor's son, the Telegraph Operator's two sons, the Ferry Man's boy and the son of a man who works for the mission! Aren't you all a bunch of idiots? I ought to throw you all in jail and throw away the key. But I won't! No sirree! I've got something worse in mind. Right now, I want each of you to go and confess to your dads what you did and get the whipping you deserve. I'll be checking to make sure you've done it. And all of you show up here tomorrow morning at nine o'clock sharp. I've got a half day's work on the wood pile for all of you."

I remember going home with very mixed emotions. I was relieved that I did not have to spend the night in jail. But, what would Doc do to me when I told him?

At last, I worked up the courage to approach him in his hospital office. Timidly, I blurted out the whole shameful story and the sentence that the policeman had passed on all of us.

As I spoke, I could see that Doc was having a struggle controlling his emotions. Was he repressing anger? But why did there seem to be laughter in his eyes?

He was content to ask a few questions of who, how and where and then I waited nervously for the anticipated blast. At last, he gained enough control to speak.

"Ne fait pas ça encore" he said as sternly as he could, then added, "et ne dit rien à ta mère."

That was all? Don't do it again and don't tell my mother? Relief flooded my entire being and I went to bed that night almost looking forward to my stint on the wood pile.

We were all there early the next day. Jean-Marie and Chummy wielded the swede saw while Jimmy chopped and Charlie and I carried and piled. None of us appeared to have suffered much from parental discipline.

Soon, we had served our sentence and were free to go home.

Of course, the whole story was a source of great amusement throughout the village. And for some unexplainable reason, I must have been tagged as the gang ring-leader. Wherever I went I was greeted with a snickering,

"Tansi, Home-Brew Bill? You gots a bottle a wine to sell me?"

All I could do was blush in embarrassment and swear at that damn Chummy under my breath!

CHAPTER 20:-A CHILD IS BORN.

Author's note: I've decided I can't be the narrator of the following story without spoiling it. Nothing should degrade the overpowering sense of aloneness that it demands. And the woman's whole life must somehow be brought into it just as she described it to me over the years when I was privileged to know her and to love her like a second mother.

Marzella Walcer felt uneasy. Despite the fact that she had become a hardened woman who could mush a team of dogs along her own line of traps or shoot and butcher a moose on the trail by herself, that unfamiliar twinge that she had felt deep in her swollen belly worried her. The brief pain had come soon after her husband, Joe, and his trapping partner, Tom Thomas, left to do a final round of their trapline north of Dipper Lake before the plane came. She had insisted that they go; that she would be alright despite her pregnant condition.

Marzella felt another knotting of her stomach. Was she going to be sick? Surely it wasn't time for the baby yet! That new Doctor in Ile a la Crosse had estimated it wouldn't be due for another three weeks or more. An aeroplane pickup was scheduled in ten days, plenty of time to get her to the hospital for pre-natal care.

But she couldn't shake the feeling of something being wrong. It was no time to be sick. Joe and Tom, she knew, would be checking traps for at least five days. She suddenly became keenly aware of her total aloneness, in their log cabin, miles and miles from another human habitation.

"Damn it Marzella!" she scolded herself, "Pull yourself together."

After all, it wasn't the first time she'd been left alone for a few days while the men were away in the bush, and she had always toughed it out and looked after herself. But she hadn't been pregnant then. For once, she was almost terrified of the fact that she was totally alone. Just then, a vision of her man, Joe, flashed in her mind and he seemed to be saying, "Do not be afraid because I'll be there soon."

Recovering herself, she decided she had better get ready, just in case. She donned her parka and mukluks, hefted the axe and headed out to the woodpile. It wasn't long before she had enough split wood piled up near the stove to last several days. What else? Water!

Grabbing the water pail and the long ice chisel, she followed the well packed trail to the frozen river and the iced over water hole.

Wielding the six foot steel bar expertly, she chipped through some 10 inches of new ice until she had a hole big enough to allow her to use the dipper to fill her bucket with.

The slight rise up the river bank on the trail back to the cabin seemed so much steeper, suddenly, and the water pail seemed so much heavier than ever before. Exhausted from her efforts, it took her last ounce of strength to open the cabin door. She felt another violent knotting in her bowels just then and as she hefted the heavy bucket up onto the wash stand, her water broke.

Nothing in Marzella's experience and upbringing had prepared her for this. In a near panic, she shrugged out of her wet trousers and underclothing. Convinced now that her situation was serious, she tried to calm herself and decide what to do.

Maybe a cup of tea would make her feel better. She built up the fire in the potbellied stove and put the kettle on to boil.

While waiting she decided, just in case, to bring her shuck filled mattress near the stove so she could more easily keep the fire going if she was laid up for a while.

She felt increasing waves of pain as she stood wondering what she should do next. Could the baby be coming already?

180

She took the First Aid book off the shelf intending to consult it.

Just then, noting the steam rising from the boiling kettle, she stepped across the bed on the floor intending to make her tea. As she did, the baby tumbled out onto the mattress.

She stood uncomprehending and in shock for several seconds until the baby's faint wail brought her back into reality.

Bending, she picked up the first aid book from where she had dropped it on the floor and leafed through it until she found the sentence that said, "If the baby is born early, the mother must stay in bed until the doctor comes." Disgusted, she flung the book across the room.

She sank down on her knees beside the infant. Noting its wet appearance, she reached for the tea towel hanging from the washstand and gently patted him clean. A boy! A baby boy! But that cord that still trailed from him to the placenta. What should she do? Instinctively she looked for something to tie it off with. The moose hide lace from her mukluk was the only thing at hand. But was it clean enough? She soaked it in the hot kettle for a minute or so. Needing something to fish the thong out of the boiled water, her eyes fell on the worn skinning knife that was always kept by the stove to cut wood shavings to start a fire with.

Using the   sterilized thong and knife she tied off and cut the cord.

This done, she felt an overpowering need to sleep. She took off the Siwash sweater she still wore over her lumberjack shirt and wrapped the baby in it. Then, holding the baby in the crook of her arm, she lay down with him and promptly lost consciousness.

Suddenly, she was at dockside in Halifax as her mother and her father, Captain Bader Perrie, waved goodbye from the top of the gangway before they left once more on another ocean voyage aboard the Steam Ship Antonia that her father commanded.

Then, little Marzella Perrie was back in her boarding school bed in the dormitory she shared with other genteel little girls, each with far away parents. The Sister who kept watch over them at night checked that all of them were tucked in, then led them in their night time prayers before snapping off the light. The same prayers, the same bed, the same routine day after day and night after night for…how many years? She tried to count them but kept getting confused.

She drifted away again and there she was in a prairie one room school facing her class of farm children ranging in size from the three little first graders to the two strapping country boys in their eighth year who towered over her.

She was saying goodbye to them for the last time and she had tears in her eyes as she watched them trudge back to their depression wracked farm homes.

Then there was Joe striding through the school yard to the school door. The tall determined young son of the Polish immigrants who had taken a homestead in the Melfort region near the Carrot River had won Marzella's heart and now, like a rustic white knight, Joe Walcer was proposing to carry her off into a frightening adventure.

"Are you ready to go?" he asked

"Just a minute Joe."

She added a few more items to the box on the teacher's desk. Then as a final act, she took down the framed photograph of her dead parents. She thought briefly of the inheritance that had frittered away to nothing trying to help her lawyer employer and other friends in Saskatoon during the early days of the depression. All for nothing, as it turned out, and she herself had been forced to find this job as a country school teacher for a subsistence salary. Fortunately, she had received free board and room with the Berhoff family who had the farm next to the Walcer farm. Both families were living on the little that the farms' gardens and chickens produced. This did allow her to save most of the little money she had made teaching. And in the process she had fallen in love with the second son of the Walcer family, Joe.

Suddenly the scene shifted again and she was sitting on a rotted stump in front of a small rough log shack. It had taken them two days of heavy going northward from the Dene village of Dipper Lake to get here. She was exhausted and she was shivering from the late Autumn cold and the snow that had begun to fall early that morning now fell so heavily that it blocked out any of the beauty that the place might have had.

"The pole roof fell in, probably last spring when Crazy Louis left the place." Joe was saying. "The cabin is totally unliveable right now so we'll have to pitch the tent for tonight."

Seeing the tears in Marzella's eyes, he quietly added, "Don't worry Dear. I'll fix it up in the morning. We can use the tent and our big tarp to fix the roof some. I'm just sorry we left so late from the farm but my Father needed help to harvest the crop, such as it was. But sweetheart, we'll make do".

Was that her crying like that? She had so tried not to show Joe her deep disappointment. Why was she crying so weakly?

She woke with a start as she realized it was a baby's cry that she was hearing. Yes the baby was crying. Was the child hungry?

What was she to do? Nothing in her convent upbringing had prepared her for motherhood.

Her eyes fell on the kettle at the back of the stove. She felt the water and found it still warm. She put a little sugar in her tea spoon and added water. Putting it to the baby's mouth she was relieved to see him suck on the sugar mixture. She had given up canned milk with her tea as it was too expensive. But she remembered a can of reindeer milk that Crazy Louis had left behind. Would that be still good? Tom Thomas had said that reindeer milk wasn't harmed by freezing. Determined to try it, carefully crawled to the shelf where she found the can and brought it back to the bed on the floor.

She managed to punch a hole in it with the knife. Smelling it and tasting it on the tip of her finger, it seemed alright. She mixed it with more of the sugar and water concoction in her enamelled tea mug and, one spoonful at a time, she fed the child until he fell asleep. She replaced the damp Siwash sweater with a makeshift diaper made of a hand towel. Then she re-wrapped him in her warm lumberjack shirt.

She kept herself and her baby alive on this reindeer milk and sugar water mixture for four days.

Out on the trap line during all this time, Joe was suffering from lack of sleep brought on by bad dreams.

In these dreams Marzella was always in eminent danger, breaking through the ice or falling off a cliff, always with himself watching the tragedy unfold but powerless to intervene. On the third night he couldn't sleep so at about 1 o'clock he woke his partner, Tom.

"I feel there's trouble at the cabin so I'm going back right away. We've still got a good two strings of traps to cover so you keep the dogs and do that. I'm going to head back on snowshoes right now because I think Marzella's having trouble of some kind."

The taciturn former British Marine never minced words. "Bout time you come to your senses. Leaving a woman in such a condition indeed! Hardly nowt in yon traps anyhows. Won't take me mor'n a day to check them."

Packing himself a sandwich Joe started out on an absolutely clear moonlit night across country. The sun was just starting to rise as he neared the cabin. There had been a light snowfall two nights before so nearing the water hole and noting no traces of footsteps leading to the cabin, he was in a panic to get to the door.

That early morning Marzella was very hungry. Except for getting the can of milk, she had obeyed the First Aid Book directions to stay in bed for now going on close to four days. There was next to nothing substantial to eat in the cabin and her

thoughts kept   wandering to the
frozen hind quarter of a moose that was on
the cabin roof, out of reach of any
passing wolverine.

She had nearly made up her mind to say to
hell with what the First Aid book said. She
was determined that she would get dressed to
go out long enough to take the axe to that
frozen meat. She was about to put her plan
into action when she heard the unmistakeable
sound of crunching footsteps approaching the
door.

For some unknown reason, she had slipped
the wooden latch that locked the cabin door
as she had come in with the water.

"Is that you Joe?" she called out weakly.
"I can't get up to open the door. Just slip
your knife through the crack and lift the
latch up."

Hearing her, Joe   heaved a shoulder
against the door and knocked it off its
leather hinges.

The sight of his wife on the floor with a
baby beside her made this strong man faint
dead away!

Marzella   could   only   stare   in
consternation at her inert husband who had
collapsed on the floor just out of her
reach. Feeling terribly weak she tried to
sit up to go to his side but couldn't.

After a minute he came to and knelt down beside her and the infant.

"Oh sweetheart," he said,"I'm so sorry you had to go through this by yourself."

"Well I wasn't really alone because I felt you were there all along" she replied. "But me and the baby are starving. Hurry up and fix us something to eat."

Tired out from sitting up and talking, she lay down again as Joe sprang into action.

Before long he had a healthy stew going on the stove and he tended to his newborn.

"There's some more reindeer milk left in the can" she explained. "I've been mixing it with hot water and sugar and feeding him by the spoonful."

Tom arrived with the dogs the next day. Joe had re-hung the door and as Tom came in carrying the frozen pelts to thaw for stretching, he was greeted with the odd sight of Marzella still on her mattress on the floor drinking tea while Joe was holding a baby trying to feed him with a contraption made from a leather glove.

Tom dropped his pelts and turned to Marzella.

"Well this is a pretty how d'you do ain't it missus? Boy or girl?"

"A skookum baby boy" Joe said carrying his son up to his partner to show him off.

"Say hello to your Uncle Tom, baby Wally" Joe said. From then on Tom was to be called Uncle Tom by all his friends.

"Joe," he said, "'member that smoke we saw down t'other side o' the lake? Might be an Indian camp where I can get help. The dogs is still hitched up so maybe I better go see right away." With this said, Tom was off leaving Joe to tend to his wife and baby.

When Tom returned nearly two hours later, he had a Dene woman with him. When she saw Joe trying to spoon feed the baby a concoction of the canned milk, she burst out laughing. Gently she took the baby to Marzella. Feeling strong enough to sit up now , Marzella understood, not the loud explanation in Dene words, but the gestures that the woman made indicating her own breasts and Marzella's and making sucking sounds pointing at the child's mouth. Soon the baby was hungrily sucking his first real meal."

Author's note: Thus did my childhood best friend and constant companion, Wally Walcer, come into our world.

When Doc eventually saw the new mother and baby, both were hale and hearty. When he heard the whole story of Marzella's pre-maternity activity with the axe and ice chisel, he was left to wonder if his estimate of the accouchement date had been so very wrong or whether the strenuous work had led to a somewhat premature birth.

From front to back: Bebe Lavoie, Wally Walcer, Marzella Walcer, Maman Lavoie, unknown, Emile and Rene. Doc was likely the photographer.

Truth to tell, Doc always had a hard time outguessing babies. They seemed to come in their own time, seldom in his. In fact when a maternity was expected, it was his habit to lie down on his bed fully clothed waiting for the electric bell to be rung by the nursing staff summoning him to the delivery room. Compared to white women, most native women had easy births and complications were rare. Despite being dressed and ready for the call bell, fairly often, the baby arrived before he did.

Two northern mothers and their bundled babies.

In fact, on one occasion, a woman showed up at the admittance desk in the hospital in very advanced labour and before little Sister Gaudette could get the mother to a bed, the baby decided to be born right there in front of the reception desk.

Summoned by the frantic bell ringing, Doc arrived to see the mother on the linoleum floor with the baby well under way, and Sister Gaudette trying to shoo away a number of the other hospital patients who had been drawn out of their rooms by all the commotion.

"Allez-vous en! Go away! Awass, awass!" she was crying in three languages gesticulating with both arms trying to create some semblance of privacy for the event.

Doc had to laugh at her embarrassed efforts, saying, "Voyons donc, ma Soeur! Je ne savais pas que tu étais trilingue." (Goodness, Sister! I didn't know you were trilingual.)

That mother and child also suffered no ill effects from their unusual birth adventure.

One other baby did test Doc's medical prowess to extremes. It was in 1946, during the hundredth anniversary celebrations of the founding of the Saint Jean Baptiste mission in Ile-a-la-Crosse. The event had drawn hundreds of people from all over the North. The village was invaded by so many clergymen, many had to be temporarily quartered in the hospital.

L to R: Emile, Rev. Father Emmanuel Paquette(Maman's brother), His Eminence Cardinal Rodrigue Villeneuve, Doctor Lavoie and Mrs. Lavoie. Kneeling in front with a clean white shirt is Bebe.

Doc and Maman had the honour of hosting the Very Reverend Cardinal Rodrigue Villeneuve, the highest ranked clerical visitor, in our spare bedroom.

Doc was busy writing his welcoming speech when a breathless young man came to fetch him.

"Some kids said they can hear a baby crying at the bottom of a toilet. We sent for the police and I came for you."

Doc and the RCMP arrived at the scene at about the same time. Hearing the unmistaken call of an infant, weak though it was, the two men managed to push over the wooden biffy. Confirming his worst fears, there was the baby lying on top of the considerable pile of excrement.

Without a moment's hesitation, Doc jumped into the hole himself, cleared the baby's face and taking off his cardigan sweater, wrapped the baby in it and handed it up to the policeman. He was helped out of the hole by several people who had gathered there out of curiosity.

As soon as he was out, Doc grabbed the baby and rushed him to the hospital for emergency care.

Doc fought to give that baby a chance, spending every spare hour ministering to his needs. I was twelve years old at the time but I was so involved with the mission centennial celebrations that I was totally unaware of the life and death struggle that Doc was involved with. Father Remi was summoned to baptise the infant right away, just in case. Not surprisingly, the child

was christened   'Rodrigue" in honour
of our eminent room guest.

Treatment went on for many weeks but,
eventually, the baby was out of danger.

Baby Rodrigue was the chief topic of
conversation in our house all the time he
was in the hospital. Maman often went to see
the child and to hold him and rock him. Doc
too was obviously very fond of the boy to
the point where he might have kept him
hospitalised   longer   than   absolutely
necessary. But I was indeed surprised when I
learned that my parents were planning to
file to adopt baby Rodrigue. Would that mean
that I was not to be called Bébé any more?

And what about baby Rodrigue's natural
mother?

I was later to learn that the frightened
teenager who chose to have her baby in that
privy and to leave it there rather than face
her parents with her "sin" was duly charged
with attempted manslaughter and served two
years, less a day, in prison. It was while
she was thus incarcerated that she signed
away her rights as the child's mother in
favour of the doctor and his wife.

Baby Rodrigue at four months old.

So, just as I was about to become a
teenager, I had a baby brother to play with
and to grow to love.

CHAPTER 21:-A CAST OF CHARACTERS.

Doc often wondered at the gallery of wonderfully strange characters that populated the north. When he himself opted to remain in the North at an inferior salary long after he could have returned to the more lucrative South, which was Maman's constant plea, he began to wonder what quirk of spirit kept him in Ile a la Crosse and his vast and nearly empty district. Had he too become a somewhat weird 'muskegger'?

I myself often wonder what continually drew me back to the wild and wondrous land of my childhood. Had I been somehow mesmerised by whistling at the dancing northern lights? This was a definite 'no no' according to northern native people.

Because, truth to tell, there were more interesting human beings per hundred square miles in the North than I ever counted elsewhere across Canada except, perhaps, in Newfoundland. And each one was good for a pleasant anecdote or a laugh.

Take the case of Abraham Ratt, for example. Doc's first encounter with "Braham" was when their individual dog teams crossed paths in the middle of Ile-a-la Crosse Lake which led to a not uncommon melée of fighting dogs. Throughout the skirmish, Braham kept yelling,

"Ha! No money. YEW yew No Money. Cowiya No money."

When 'Braham and Montagnais, Doc's dog driver, finally succeeded in separating and calming the dogs, Doc had to ask,

"Why you say many times, 'no money'?

"Oh, that the name of my lead dog," was the answer.

Thinking this a rather strange name for a dog, Doc had to ask,

"Why you call your dog No Money for goodness sakes?"

"Well, because he didn't cost me anything," was 'Braham's logical, if peculiar, reply.

Doc was still chuckling about the encounter when he got home and told us about a dog called No Money.

Naturally, like any curious kid bent on making fun of such a thing, when I myself saw Braham and his dog team at the HBC store, I couldn't resist asking,

"Why do you call your dog No Money?"

The answer I got froze the laugh in my throat.

"Because that damn dog not worth nothing. He is such a poor lead dog.

Abraham Ratt's dog team with "NO MONEY" leading.

I came to learn that 'Braham had more
answers regarding his dog's peculiar name
than No Money had fleas. He might say he was
called No Money because he was such a good
dog that he would not sell him for any
money. Or maybe it was because he had stolen
the dog because he couldn't pay for it. Or
yet again because when that dog howled at
night, it sounded like he was yelling
'nooooo moooonieeeeeeeee'!

'Braham was a natural comedian. When I
asked him once what kind of pelt I saw on
top of his cariole pack, he told me it was a
'pitzue' skin, or what whites called a lynx,
the only member of the cat family in that
area.

He couldn't   resist asking me, "Bébé, you know why in Cree he is called pitzue?" When I shook my head to indicate my ignorance he went on to say,

"Well it is because when lynx get caught in trap and you come near he always snarl 'pits on you' and dat what he try to do. Hee hee hee!"

Some of the most bizarre people were the whites who came north and got "bushed" as the saying went. One of the most magnificent and most bizarre was certainly the missionary priest, Father Moreau. What a man he was! Arriving from Quebec with only one language, French, he threw himself zealously into learning the Cree language. He ministered to several Cree missions for a few years until, as Doc liked to explain, the Cree and Métis became too civilized for him. So he pestered his bishop to send him among the Chipewyans who spoke the Dene Language, a very complex and tongue twisting language. Père Moreau attacked this second native language with his customary ferocity and soon he could preach a sermon in Dene for over an hour without notes.

He must have begun to think of himself as a natural linguist because he decided to tackle English next, the dominant language of northern commerce. With the help of schoolbooks and the CBC, he did manage after a while to speak some passable, though often inaccurate English.

199

Rev. Father R.P.L. Moreaud, O.M.I., one of the most energetic missionaries in the north in Doc's day.

One time Doc was visiting Father Bourbonnais in Buffalo Narrows. This priest had been sent to Buffalo Narrows specifically because he spoke good English. The opening of the fish processing plant there had brought in quite a number of English speakers from the south.

"Ah Docteur Lavoie," he greeted Doc, "it is a good thing you came as I need your opinion. I received this week a note from Father Moreau in Patuanak which I show you. Would you think that this is a clerical or a medical observation?"

Doc read the note   and   burst   out laughing for it read,

"Dear   Father   Bourbonnais.   I
write to tell you that there is
nothing on the way for Angelique
Lariviere from my mission to get
married to your young man Etienne
Bilette."

Many Dene elders remember Père Moreau more with awe than with fondness for he was a demanding martinet who might show up at your cabin door some morning commanding you to hitch up your dogs immediately and take him down river to one of his several satellite missions. And he considered himself the final word about what a baby would be named at its baptism. Yet they knew that the good Father would starve himself first before seeing one of his people go hungry.

And he was a consummate, and devious, bum. If he saw you boating on the lake he would invariably wave you down from his canoe and upon approaching he might say,

"I do not think I have enough gasoline to get to Ile a la Crosse. You could perhaps spare me a little bit?"

There would be several twenty gallon drums in the bottom of his boat, obviously full of mixed gas. But, with a helpless shrug, you would top up the tank on his kicker knowing that he was saving his hoard to give to his parishioners if they needed it to go hunting or fishing.

And he loved to bum rides on an aeroplane no matter where it was going. One early fall day when the good Father was visiting in Ile a la Crosse, he learned that Doc had chartered a flight to Cree Lake. He immediately rushed down to the plane wharf.

"Eh, monsieur pilote, I have need to get to Cree Lake to visit my families there. Can I catch it a ride with you and the Docteur?"

Bill Windrum of M and C aviation knew it would be useless to say no.

"Well, Father, I guess I can squeeze you on. But I'm pretty heavy loaded so it will have to be just you and your bedroll, you understand."

"Ah but I gots some very nice potatoes here at the mission. Surely only one bag of potatoes would not be too much," pleaded the priest. "Those families at Cree Lake have nothing save fish to eat."

"No Father! I told you, just you and your bedroll. I'll be overloaded as it is," the pilot insisted.

"Eh bien!. Very well. I will be back very soon with my bedroll" and he went running up the hill to the rectory.

Before long he was back at the wharf accompanied by Brother Loranger pushing a wheelbarrow containing just a bedroll. His suspicions piqued, Bill Windrum stopped the Missionary Brother as he was about to lift the bedroll off the wheelbarrow and he insisted on putting it on the plane himself.

He nearly strained his back hefting the bedroll!

"What the heck have you got rolled up in here, Father?" he asked and he unrolled the bundle to reveal some fifty pounds of spuds.

Father Moreaud and his potatoes did not fly to Cree Lake that day.

Was he a saint? Perhaps. When he died the Dene people of Patuanak demanded that he be buried behind their church and they built a shrine in his honour over his grave.

Some of the most fun people were the non-native trappers, a few of whom had come North, I learned, to avoid wartime service.

One such, I think, was big Joe Buckley of the loud voice. He would have made a heck of a good drill sergeant in the army, had he signed up, as his normal voice level was a booming roar.

When he was returning to Ile-a-la-Crosse from his trap line at Keller Lake way down the Churchill River, you could hear him yelling from miles away,

"Sit still you bloody mutts or I'll hit you over the head with a paddle!"

There was a good reason for this verbal abuse of his dogs. His canoe, barely measuring twelve feet, full of his winter's catch and all his equipment would have been close to swamping as it was. Yet on top of this load were his four sled dogs, trembling in abject terror. There could not have been much more than an inch of freeboard keeping Buckley from a wet backside. But he always managed to beach his cargo, safe and dry.

It became Joe Buckley's practice to leave his dogs in the care of my brothers, René and Emile near the Fort Black mink ranch that they operated at the south end of the lake. There the dogs lived on scrap fish not fit for the minks. Meanwhile, Buckley went south to sell his winter's catch of fur. It wasn't long before he returned with a moon sized hangover and empty pockets. But he always came back with one bottle of Hudson Bay rum that he needed to sweeten up his snuff. He also had several cases of relatively cheap "crack" eggs to feed to his dogs along with their diet of fish. On this regimen, they grew fat and sleek over the summer months so that they were in great shape for their winter's mushing when they were paddled back to Keller Lake in the fall.

A fairly adept carpenter, Buckley spent the summer working at the Fort Black mink ranch building shelters and individual pens for the spring's production of mink pups.

Once weaned and   each in an individual pen they would grow to pelting size by late Autumn.

As I was out of school for summer vacation, it became my dubious assignment to help Buckley with his work. I was subject to a stream of loud commands and to occasional ridicule which bothered me at first.

"Dontcha know the difference between a two by four and a one by six for krissakes? And square that board before giving it to me."

But over time I became used to his bluster and learned the basics of working with wood.

"Measure twice and cut once. Get your damn fingers away from the saw. You may need all ten some day. Let the hammer do the work and you won't bend so many nails. How many board feet of shiplap will we need to roof that new mink shed? Here's how you figure it out."

At night, after supper, he would light his pipe and entertain us with an endless stream of stories. His favourite subject was about how tough and strong his friend and fellow trapper Ed Theriault was.

"You know, one time I met Ed on the Dipper portage when I was going in to the post for tobacco.

Damn if that   sonofagun didn't have a full sized cook stove strapped to his back!"

"Where the hell are you going with that bloody cook stove?" I asks him.

"Oh, my new wife Evange has been complaining that she can't cook decent on my old pot bellied stove so I'm taking this one up to Endless Lake." He answers me.

"Well, put that load down for a while and rest your back," I says.

"Thanks Buckley," he says, "but if I put it down I'll just have to go to the trouble of loading it back on again. But if you want to help me out, could you open the oven door and check that fifty pound sack of flour I've got in there? I think it may have shifted to the left a bit."

Famed trapper Ed Theriault and his admirer, Joe Buckley playing a game of crib and swapping yarns.

"That gaddam Ed Theriault is one strong sonovabitch".

At the end of summer, I was actually sad to see my carpentry instructor paddle away with his fattened dog team trembling on top of his winter's supplies.

"First one of you damn dogs moves is gonna end up swimmin' to Keller Lake!"

But the person who became my alter grandfather, my 'moshôm', Clément Roy, tops my list of memorable characters. He had been hired as a fisherman to help lift the many nets that feeding 1500 or more minks demanded over the summer. But Clément refused to use an outboard motor on his skiff, insisting on using his oars no matter how far he had his sets.

My oldest brother René, who considered himself the main man of fish, complained ceaselessly about how long it took Clément to bring in his catch. But the old fellow kept his job even when he went on an occasional bender. Why? Because when everyone else was pulling up near empty nets in August, Clément invariably knew where the fish were, and never came back without his usual full tubs.

Whenever I could escape the work demands of my brothers, I loved to go along with my moshôm in his fishing skiff. I learned much in that rowboat. I learned the habits of every type of water-fowl. The pelicans

especially must have   learned to recognise
the squeak of his oars, or the smell of his
pipe tobacco mixed with kinikinik bark
because they were always there, wherever we
went. And as he lifted the nets, he would
throw any sucker fish to them one by one. He
gave them names like "p'ti vieux' or 'gros
bec', and they seemed to respect the order
of precedence that he accorded each one.

Le vieux Clement Roy, my adoptive moshom. A
great man who always knew where to find fish.

One evening, Clément announced that he
and I were going to go get some ducks the
next morning, as he was getting tired of a
steady diet of the three B's, i.e. bannock,
bacon and beans.

I had barely closed my eyes in sleep when I felt his gentle shake and heard his whispered,

"Astum Bébé, the sisipuk will be flying in soon."

It was still pitch black as I followed the old man to the familiar rowboat. He handed me our old single shot twelve gauge shotgun and four shells to hold as he got his oars set up.

"Only four shells?" I couldn't help asking.

"Kwêyikohk, that's all we'll need," he stated.

I couldn't help but wonder how he would feed five men on just four ducks. I had regularly stuffed away two birds at a sitting myself in the past.

The sun was just beginning to rise as we pulled into a small back-water behind the Fort. Carefully, Clément positioned the skiff in some tall reeds near the shore.

It wasn't long before the first flight of ducks splashed in for a landing. I expected the old man to shoulder the shotgun in readiness but he just sat there, cleaning and refilling his pipe.

As more and more ducks came in, the suspense and waiting for something to happen

was too much for me   and   I   pointed
excitedly at a couple of nearby mallards,

"Magana sisipuk, nimoshôm!" I whispered
as if the old man's eyes and ears had failed
to notice the obvious presence of the ducks.

But all Clément did was put a silencing
finger to his lips as he continued
ministering to his pipe.

At long last, he rose up in the boat,
shouldered the gun and fired. Then we rowed
out and picked up the five dead birds
floating in the water.

Back again in our reed hideaway we once
more waited for the ducks to form up on the
water into a tight group within our range
and "bang'! Seven ducks with the second
shell!

He didn't even have to fire the fourth
shell because after the third shot we
counted a total of sixteen ducks in the
bottom of the boat, which we considered
enough. Waste not, want not!

But the lesson wasn't over until I had
been taught how to properly pluck and singe
the birds ready for cooking.

I learned more about the wonder of life
from that patient and wise elder than I have
from every professor I have heard and every
book I have read.

If Doc were to contribute to this cast of memorable characters, he probably would choose to include Mistadoo, the medicine woman.

Mistadoo was both respected and feared by northern people; respected for her vast knowledge of medicinal herbs and fungi, feared because of her legendary powers to cast spells on or for her clients.

To Doc the medicine woman was an enigma, a combination of proven traditional knowledge and occultist beliefs. Though he jokingly referred to her as his colleague, he recognised her capabilities with natural medicines; rat root to ease congestion of the throat, a poultice of yarrow to treat infected wounds, and so on. But when anyone mentioned the power of Mistadoo's concoction of 'love medicine' Doc would only snort in disbelief. Yet even an educated European like George Walker swore that a certain lady had ensnared him with a draught of love medicine in his tea, and no matter how hard he tried to break the spell, he was inexorably hooked.

It became Doc's standard practice to ask his older native patients if they were being treated by Mistadoo and if so with what, before prescribing treatment for fear of complications. For example, a herb that Mistadoo used to treat heart sickness, he discovered, had similar chemical properties to digitalis.

Despite my cowering fear of Mistadoo's powers, I myself came very close to becoming a client of the witch doctor when I became a horny teenager.

I had just turned fifteen when Marcien Marion hired a young beauty from Prince Albert to clerk in his store over the summer. Her name shall remain locked in my breast. Not only was she attractive in the extreme, but she actually used makeup like the movie stars pictured in the Liberty Magazine. On top of all that, she had a voice that stroked your ears like velvet, and a smile that seemed to instantly convey a message of, "I like you" to whomever she faced.

I fell totally, helplessly under her spell. I became like an addict needing a daily hormonal jolt, scrabbling to find the two bits I needed to buy a bottle of Orange Crush from Marion's pop cooler, so I could legitimately hang around the store for hours as the drink grew warm in my hand and the sight of her was branded more deeply into my swollen heart.

One day, I found out that the next day was to be her birthday. Immediately I was convinced that I had to use that occasion to my advantage if I was to win her affection. But what could a penniless young swain do to impress this goddess? I spent a sleepless night considering every possibility from robbing the Church Collection box to armed hold-up of the HBC. In the end, I chose the

one most perfect rose that Maman had
been nurturing in her flower garden for some
coming saint's feast day, and smuggled it
hidden in my zippered sweater to Marion's
store.

I blushingly handed the rose to my lady
as I stammered "Happy Birthday".

Her delight in my gesture was genuine,
and she kissed me full on the lips. Yes! She
kissed me! Oh scrabgeous day, callou,
calley! Tears of joy pushed at my eyes and I
had to rush outdoors to hide my unmanliness
and to savour the feeling of that silken
touch that so vibrated still on my mouth. I
was transported into a world full of music
and light and the glorious subtle smell of
her perfume.

I dared to think that she was to be mine
alone.

Imagine my consternation that very night,
a movie night, when she came to the hall in
the company of my older brother, Emile. They
sat right in front of me and as the hall
darkened and the first reel flickered onto
the screen, I saw her shamelessly drawing
closer and closer to my traitor brother. And
then when Emile put his arm around her
shoulder, she wickedly snuggled her head
against his chest. The hurt was so great
that for the first time in my young life, I
left the movie before it had barely started
and sought the secrecy of the darkest place

I could find where my tears contended with my fiery anger for supremacy.

And that is when, in that moment of mad emotions, I resolved to seek the help of the occult.

So the very next day, after several false starts, I finally got up enough courage to approach Mistadoo's door.

"Kekway n'dawithtamin Mestigosew?" she gently asked me what I wanted.

Afraid to look her in the eye, I asked her how much it would cost to get some love medicine from her.

She didn't answer me right away and when I looked to see if she had understood what I had said, she was nodding her head and smiling.

"It will cost you nothing," she told me in French, "on one condition. You must bring me a note from your father, the doctor, saying that he agrees to let me give you the medicine you want."

Of course, I couldn't do that! So my love was left to wither and die like a purloined rose.

CHAPTER 22:-DEATH AS PART OF LIFE.

Two images are burned in startling detail in my memory. One was watching my grand-father, Pé-Père Lavoie, in his death throes. Doc had taken me and my two brothers to the hospital to bid Pé-Père our final farewells. It was soon obvious that the old man was beyond even recognizing our presence. What fascinated me and scared me were the vigorous movements of his arms as he lay in his hospital bed, as if he was shadow boxing a being on the ceiling.

I grabbed Doc's hand in fear and in a whisper asked him why Pé-Père was acting this way.

He answered that maybe the old man was trying to frighten death away, or maybe he was battling the devil.

Was death so frightening then? I wondered. I knew that Father Rossignol had just preceded our visit to give the old man the last sacraments. Wasn't it the priest's job to keep the devil at bay?

The second personal experience of death was the day I watched a little native girl that I knew from school being pulled out of the water, feet first, and heard her dead body thump as it hit the bottom of the mission boat. Soon after, I watched the men in the boat draw up the form of a nun, still dressed in her heavy   brown habit that now clung to her like a wet blanket.

Her black wimple had come away from her head in her struggle to save the drowning girl. She had lost her own life in the vain attempt.

It wasn't unusual for the Sisters to take small groups of residential school children to that beach for a swim in the heat of a June Day. I had swum there myself so often, without fear, that I had a hard time understanding how the tragic double drowning could have happened. It was my older brother René who provided the explanation. The little girl couldn't swim well and had gotten out beyond her depth. There was a steep drop off about there and none of the other girls were brave enough to answer the girl's cries for help so the Sister had waded in fully dressed and had been pulled down in her turn into deep water.

I remember crying and being pretty angry at God for letting this happen.

Doc, who had tried every resuscitation technique he knew on the two victims, and failed, was also visibly shaken. The death of children, I had come to know, bothered him terribly. He tried to comfort me by telling me that both the little girl and the Sister were now in a happy place in Heaven because they had never been very bad.

In time, as I attended the wakes that normally preceded funerals, where the dead body would lie open to the view of every one in the community for up to three days, I learned to lose my fear of the dead.

But the uncertainty of the kind of life after death that I might expect troubled me. How good did you have to be to go to heaven? For a while I went to confession every chance I got for fear I might have lost my laissez-passer by some little misdemeanour. But when I eventually learned that one could get in if one said an act of contrition at the last minute before death, my tension eased off considerably.

In time, I learned not to think of death at all. Others died, but not me.

The saddest death, Doc insisted, would be one where the dying person would go through the ordeal alone. One such death resulted in the following statements taken by the R.C.M.P. from A.B. Bjerga's poignant diary in which he recounts day by day the growing weakness that his illness caused and his acceptance that he would soon die alone in his trapper's cabin in the late winter of 1937. The following is copied verbatim from the Royal Canadian Mounted Police report regarding Mr. Bjerga's death.

ROYAL   CANADIAN   MOUNTED POLICE

Ile a la Crosse

May 26, 1937.

Re: Asbjorn Bernhard BJERGA Deceased

Clearwater River, Sask.

   COPY OF STATEMENTS OF THE ABOVE NAMED DECEASED TAKEN FROM HIS DIARY:-

BEGINS:

"April 11th ,37.

For the benefit of R.C. Mounted Police

   The first I felt anything wrong was March 11th.I was in cross the river and in past the lake 1/2mile. That trip made my feet awfull tired, and at the same time my gums swelled up, and several teet got loos. I figured then it was scurvy. I had just a few dried carrots, which I soaked in water and ate raw. I was still taxing myself and running traps, mostly for squirrels, rabbits and partridges. On April 2nd I had to give up entirely moving around anyplace. There was no difference between which foot was the worst for a long time. I was rubbing them with linement every day. Nothing helps, it was from the knee and down in the ankels first. Then my right knee started getting blue mostly on the inside tovards the other foot as well as behind. The worst place being the underside of the knee and the muscles down the leg. It don't act like Blood Poison to my knowledge. It is blue, but nothing

*red, there is red streaks   with Blood Poison. I am
getting poisoned just the same. It is getting blue now
under both arms and the other foot has also got it on
the big muscles on the hip bone. Terrible pain as soon
as I rais up, and my heart is getting awfull weak. Was
picking cranberries, as soon as I could get at them.
But no benefit in them. I am just waiting for my death
call, and I hope this book and the other records over
at Norstrom, will be sent to Jacobine Bjerga,
Skudenes, Norway. Also notice be given to Herbert E.
Hadley, Old Nat. Bank Building, Nevada, Iowa. Would
like to be buried in the Graveyard at Ile a la Crosse if
it can be arranged, and these petty debts, Ted
Figeland $10.00 Dore Lake, Frank Mitchel $5.00,
"Little Cry" Buffalo River $6.00. I don't know how far
my belongings will reach, and I am*

*afraid I will have to die in the sleeping robe and
spoil it."*

April 8ᵗʰ.

*"By all means, notify Herbert E. Hadley. Old Nat.
Bank Building, Nevada, Iowa. If I am found dead here,
which is what I expect will happen.*

A.B.B."

*"Please get my Dayly records sent to my mother
in Norway. This one and some at Einar Norstrom's
place. Some of them are funny looking, but that was
when I was short on paper."*

219

"Frank Mitchel, should have $5.00 and Theodore Figeland, Dore Lake should have $10.00 if there is anything left. Would like they were paid if possible."

"There is some daily records over at Einar Norstroms camp as well as this one. Would like to have them sent to Mrs. Jacobine Bjerga, Skudenes, Norway. In case of Death, please notify, Herbert E. Hadley, Old Nat.Bank Building, Nevada, Ia. I don't feel now as I am going to live very long, and I cannot get out"

ENDS

As Coroner, Doc had read the diary describing in heart wrenching details the Norwegian's last days on earth. Doc noted that the hand writing became more and more shaky and labored with each passing day.

Doc confirmed that the cause of death was, in fact, scurvy which is caused by a lack of vitamin C. The frozen cranberries Bjerga had dug out of the snow would have helped prevent the disease if eaten sooner and in greater quantities. It was a pity, Doc thought, that the poor fellow had not known enough to boil up some spruce or jackpine needles, and drink the resulting vitamin C rich broth. He made it a point from then on to advise all trappers to include dried or canned citrus and other fruits in their grubstakes and to take a daily dose of cod liver oil as part of their diet. It was perhaps due to his efforts that there were no further deaths as a result of scurvy during his northern service.

Joe Walcer, Marzella's husband, had very nearly died at their trapper's cabin north of Dipper Lake a few years after their Wally was born. He had suffered severe abdominal pains which suddenly stopped to be replaced by nausea and other symptoms of a burst appendix. Marzella and the partner, Tom Thomas, loaded Joe into a cariole and she mushed him to Patuanak where Father Moreau arranged for the fastest dog team in the hamlet to take the patient non-stop to the Ile-a-la-Crosse hospital. Alerted by the HBC radio, Doc had the surgery ready and waiting when the patient arrived.

The onset of peritonitis was already evident when Doc opened Joe Walcer up. With sulpha drugs used liberally and drains that had to be moved every few hours. Doc managed to pull him through but Joe spent 19 days in hospital recuperating.

Modern readers may need to understand how poor communication was between isolated cabins and the nearest facilities. Fortunately, the Walcer family knew enough to recognize the symptoms of appendicitis and to take such means as they had to get Joe to a hospital as quickly as they could. As it was it took two days of solid mushing to get him there. Doc felt that one more day may have put the case beyond help. Thus another Bjerga tragedy was averted. But what if Walcer, like Bjerga, had been alone, without a wife and partner to help him. Would he have been able to get to help on his own?

The Walcer and Lavoie families became very good friends as a result of that close call. Perhaps it was partly to get nearer to medical and other services that Joe and Marzella decided to leave their isolated trap lines and to go into mink ranching just halfway between Buffalo Narrows and Ile a la Crosse. Their only son, Wally, was of school age then and was boarded out in Buffalo to attend school about the same time I was in attendance in Ile-X.

Bebe, Emile and Wally at the Walcer mink ranch.

We saw a lot of each other during holidays. In fact, I regularly spent a couple of weeks every summer dodging Marzella's goats which provided the milk she thought her family needed.

Bush pilot Ernie Buffa regaled all listeners with the story of flying those two frisky goats in the second cockpit of a Tiger Moth from Big River to the Walcer ranch.

Ernie Buffa and his Tiger Moth. His motto became, "I'll fly anything anywhere, except goats."

One result of that friendship was the decision to send Wally Walcer and I South to boarding schools together for our junior and senior high school education. We spent two years in the little Saint Louis College in Moose Jaw for our seventh and eighth grades and then were sent to Campion College in Regina for grades nine to twelve. I will not dwell on those six years as they constitute quite a separate story. But each time I returned home to Ile a la Crosse, I was shocked to see my parents changing so much with each passing year. Doc especially seemed to be losing his vitality, his 'joie de vivre' as he aged. Truth is, I just had not been aware of his aging when we spent each year together. What Doc hid from me and perhaps from everybody else was that he was suffering from an ailing heart.

In the summer of 1952, I graduated from Campion with senior matriculation, and with Doc's blessing and evident pride, I entered 1st year Pre-Med at the University of Saskatchewan.

Doc should have retired in 1952 when he turned 65. But the government could find no one to replace him right away and evidently he wasn't anxious to leave the life he had grown accustomed to.

In 1953, the Saskatchewan Health department hired two German émigré doctors, first a Doctor Hoenig who didn't last and then a Doctor Hoffman who did.

Doc and Maman moved to Meadow Lake in the autumn of 1953. He had a small private practice there to supplement his miniscule pension. He did deliver Mrs. Bear's triplets and assisted other Meadow Lake doctors. But his own health was such that he could not do too much and had to turn away some of the Cree Indian and Métis clients there who sought him out particularly because of the high regard "Maskikhiwino Lavoie" enjoyed among the aboriginal population in the North.

As for me, I had really enjoyed my year at the University of Saskatchewan 1952/1953. Too much so! Freed at last from the controls and discipline of the Jesuit Fathers at Campion College, in Saskatoon I neglected such mundane things as lectures, library assignments and general study in favour of frolics and fun. I was in that year's production of the operetta, "Finian's Rainbow"; I won the best actor award in Saint Thomas More College's entry in the College Nights Drama Competition; I sang in the Newman Glee Club chorus. I became a very proficient Ping-Pong player.

As for pre-med studies, I loved the English and History classes but found the science classes baffling and boring. I never did learn how to balance a chemical equation nor could I find and correctly label the interior parts of the frog. I knew how to snare, skin and cook a rabbit but could not find its occipital nerve on the biology lab table.

Not surprisingly, I received a letter from the Dean of Arts and Science in May of 1953 suggesting that perhaps a Medical Degree might be somewhat beyond my capabilities. I was directed to take a year off to think it over.

I spent that spring and summer working at the mink ranch, ashamed to talk to Doc about my failure. As September approached, I had to face the reality that working for my brothers for board and room was a dead end road. René's wife, Terry, a former teacher, suggested a possibility. The Meadow Lake School Division was having trouble staffing its rural schools and was inviting applications from "suitable" high school graduates to take positions as un-licensed teachers.

The   Superintendent   of
the MLSD accepted me and I was driven by the
"helping teacher", Esther O'Connel, a dear
understanding lady, to the rural one room
school of Ferris, about an hour from Meadow
Lake. She gave me a pile of Correspondence
School self-study courses for the older kids
from 4th to 9th grades but explained that, as
they couldn't read, I would have to teach
the   primary   grades,   including   three
beginners, the fundamentals of reading and
arithmetic on my own hook. When she saw the
frightened look on my face at this prospect,
she made me sit down and write, step by
step, how to teach little kids without
frightening them too much.

Thank God for the generosity and
tolerance of farm raised kids. With their
help, I learned to cope reasonably well
before too long. In fact I grew to like
helping children learn and we enjoyed having
fun together.

But the lonely nights by myself in that
little teacherage were very difficult. It
got so that, come the weekends, I hitched
rides into Meadow Lake with whoever was
going. Thus I spent most Friday and Saturday
nights with Maman and Doc in their little
apartment. As Maman continued her habit of
really early to bed, Doc and I spent long
evenings   talking   about   anything   and
everything. I learned of his having come
west from Rimouski Quebec as a youth, of his
"proving   a   homestead"   near   Vonda
Saskatchewan with his two brothers.

Fortunately, his brothers convinced him he was not cut out for farming and insisted he go back East and finish his medical studies which he did. He confessed that he too had risked failure partying with his college buddies. But he had smartened up in time and eventually was granted his M.D.

One night, he asked me if I liked teaching, and when I admitted that I did, he pressed me into revealing what I planned to do.

I had, in fact, taken the step of enrolling in a Psychology course by correspondence, hoping thereby to fill in the long evenings in the teacherage and, perhaps, help me regain entry to university.

So I admitted to Doc that I was saving as much of my teaching income as I could so I could try Pre-Med once again. I finally found the courage to beg his forgiveness for having wasted all the money he had spent on that misspent year.

And why was I then planning to repeat that mistake, he asked me. He went on to insist that I should do what attracted me, rather than try to please him. If I enjoyed teaching, why not pursue that profession? Surely, being a teacher was as honourable as being a doctor. He pointed out that my top marks in English and History, as well as my success in dramatics, marked me as a humanist, not a scientist.

He convinced me. That spring, I applied to and was accepted by the College of Education for the fall term.

Before I left for Saskatoon, Doc asked me if I would like to accompany him on a trip to Ile a la-Crosse. Hugh Brander, the freighter in whose truck we'd hitched a ride, was to remark later what a change he noticed in Doc as we travelled the rough road north. He had sat morose and quiet when the trip started. But he smiled as we crossed the Cowan, Beaver and Waterhen rivers. He glowed with pleasure as we went through Beauval. By the time Lac Ile-a-la Crosse came into view at Fort Black he was once more his old self, remarking on the beauty of the early fall colours and recounting stories of past adventures experienced during his nearly twenty years of life in this wild and beautiful country.

We spent two days at the Fort Black Mink Ranch with René, Therese and Emile. As we crossed the lake for a visit to the hospital and to see some of his old friends, his evident pleasure was wonderful to see, and that is the way I like to remember him.

The return to Meadow Lake came all too soon. And Doc once more seemed to have lost zest for life.

My second attempt at a university education was more disciplined and therefore more successful. The generic "Education" classes were boring in the extreme, but I did manage to get into one challenging English class and the class in Ed Psych wasn't too bad.

When I went to spend the Christmas break with my parents, I couldn't get over how Doc's health had deteriorated. I was relieved to hear that René was to drive him south for a full check-up in Saskatoon's Saint Paul's Hospital in February. It was then that I had one last visit with him while he was hospitalised.

The hospital released him after only two days of testing which, in hindsight, was an ominous sign of his true condition. On the way back home, they stopped to visit René's in-laws in Prudhome for a day or two. On the Sunday morning, Doc didn't feel up to going to Mass and decided to get more bed-rest. When Maman returned from the Church service, he was gone into his eternity.

Doc had insisted that he was to be buried in his beloved village. René's wife, Therese, made all the arrangements. The word spread throughout the network of northern missions so that as the funeral cortege came across the ice road from Fort Black, hundreds of people had lined the passage that led off the lake.

The following tribute reprinted from the **Island Breezes of Feb-March 1954** describes far better than I could, the demonstration of the deep affection that northerners held for Doc.

2.

Pioneer Doctor is mourned

The news of Doctor P. E. Lavoie's death on February 17 brought sadness to the Islanders with whom he had lived in such close cooperation and entente for well-nigh twenty years.

Doctor Lavoie came North with his family in the hard '30's. Through trying hardships he earned a living for his loved ones and served the northern population. His untiring devotedness, his innumerable trips by canoe, or dog-train (before the advent of the plane, speedboat and snowbug) won him the affection and esteem not only of the Metis and Indians but of all who benefitted from his knowledge and skill.

It was during these years too that Doctor Lavoie became gradually more attached to his beloved North and its people. When, with World War II, came opportunities for better-paid, more socially attractive, more advantageous positions, Doc deliberated at length and chose to STAY. Thus he gave up his own personal worldly advancement, comfort and satisfaction in order to help his dear northerners. By this complete self-sacrifice, the bond of love between Doc and the North was greatly strengthened and when in the spring of 1953 Doctor Lavoie left his post of Medicine Man of the region extending from Water Hen to Cree Lake, he did so with deep regret. His sorrow was still greater when he definitely left Ile à la Crosse to resume the practice of his noble profession in Meadow Lake in July 1953. That seemed to mark the 'beginning of the end'. His heart condition which had been troubling him during the last few years soon became alarming.

In early February, Doctor Lavoie was admitted as a patient at St. Paul's Hospital in Saskatoon. Even the best of care and attention could bring no lasting results. To everyone's consternation, less than twenty-four hours after his discharge

from that institution, Doctor Philippe Ernest Lavoie had 3.
suddenly but very peacefully passed away on the morning of
February 17, 1954. At the time, Doctor and Mrs. Lavoie were
at the home of Mr. and Mrs. C. M. Le Page in Prud'homme
where they had stopped on their way back to their home in
Meadow Lake.

Messages by wire and radio soon spread the news far and
near. The members of his family, Mrs. D. Churnside from Ottawa, René and wife(Thérèse Le Page) and Emile from Ile à la
Crosse, and Germain from Meadow Lake rushed to join their
mother.

In response to Dr. Lavoie's last wishes, his body was
brought back to Ile à la Crosse for funeral services and
burial. Laurenti Hall was temporarily transformed into a
funeral chapel. Through the afternoon and evening of the
19th, the northerners came to pay tribute to their beloved
Pioneer Doctor and to pray for the repose of his soul.

On the morning of the 20th, funeral services were held
in St. John the Baptist Church which had donned its new
mourning apparel. The Northerners flocked from the Ile and
neighbouring hamlets. Even Prud'homme had its representa-
tives: Mrs. C. M. Le Page and her son Wilfred (Mother and
brother of Mrs. R. Lavoie) and Mrs. Eveline Loiselle, a
niece of Dr. Lavoie.

Reverend Father L. Poirier officiated at the solemn
Requiem Mass, assisted by Rev. G. Beaudet and R. Lemay as
deacon and sub-deacon. Also taking place in the sanctuary
were Rev. M. Rossignol, Snake Lake; N. Guilloux, Ile à la
Crosse; M. Landry, Beauval Residential School; J. E. Per-
reault, Beauval Village. The children's choir, aided by the
Sisters' performed beautifully.

The pall-bearers were Alex Campbell, Patuanak; Louis
Durocher, Beauval; George McCallum, Louis Desjarlais, John
Stoeber, and Ed. Gervais, all of Ile à la Crosse.

The whole ceremony was a touching expression of sincere
gratitude and love. The numerous congregation accompanied
the beloved Doctor to his last resting place beside his own
father in the local cemetery and with one heart all implored
"Everlasting Rest and Peace" for the soul of Doctor Lavoie.

God calls our loved ones, but we lose not wholly
What He hath given;
They live on earth in thought and deed as truly
As in his heaven.

Whittier.

But the last words of this story belong to Doc himself as he wrote his farewell to his beloved North and its people. (Re-typed from the May 1953 edition of Island Breezes)

" I like to remember, as well, the courtesy of the natives for myself, in the hospital and in their homes. They were always willing to accept treatment, even surgical ones, no fuss, no recriminations, no hysteria, but a stoic behaviour in pain and adversity. On a journey their attention to my welfare was very considerate, the best place in the canoe, carrying my luggage in the portages, having me well wrapped in the sleeping robe in the toboggan, the best place near the fire, the best corner of the floor for my bed, the best morsel of food, so much that I have learned to love them like brothers and I won't be able to forget them. Of course they are not perfect. Who of the white is perfect?

I will also keep a good souvenir of all my friends, the white men, the missionaries, and the Grey Nuns who have helped me so much in my task.

I will always recall the beauty and the scenery of the bush. It brings peace to life, no turmoil, no noise. The trees, the birds, the wild game, the fishing, the lakes, the rivers, the boating, there is nothing artificial. Of course it is cold here in the winter. What about it? One gets used to it. Had I my choice I would live the rest of my life in this friendly North!"

Philippe E. Lavoie , M.D.

The medicine man's son agrees whole heartedly.

THE LAVOIE GRAVE SITE IN THE ILE A LA
CROSSE GRAVEYARD, THE SMALLER STONE MARKS
DOC LAVOIE'S FATHER'S GRAVE. HIS ONLY
DAUGHTER CECILE'S ASHES ARE ALSO INTERED
THERE.

REFERENCES:

What Doc didn't tell me about the 1930s I got from reading Pierre Burton's excellent book, *The Great Depression.*

For some background details of early northern aviation the informative book *Wings Beyond Road's End* published by the Pahkisimon Nuyeh>ah Library System was helpful.

The *Island Breezes,* the little monthly news magazine produced by the teachers of the Ile-a-la-Crosse school in that era was my most valuable resource.